5 STEPS TO HEALING YOUR HEART

by Pamela Hart

Copyright © 2015 by Pamela Hart

All rights reserved. No part of this book may be reproduced or transmitted in any form or by any means, electronic or mechanical, including photocopying, recording, or by an information storage and retrieval system, without permission in writing from the publisher. Except in the case of brief quotations embodied in critical articles and reviews. For information please address Pamela Hart P.O. Box 2066, Wichita Falls TX 76307

Pamela Hart books may be purchased for educational, business, or sales promotional use. For information please write Special Markets Department, Pamela Hart P.O. Box 2066, Wichita Falls TX 76307

Table of Contents

Dedication 5

Acknowledgements by Pamela Hart 6

Forward by Dr. Karen Hollie &

Life Coach Star L. Williams 7

Preface by Pamela Hart 9

Introduction by Pamela Hart 18

Step 1-*Get Up In Forgiveness* 25

Step 2-*Get Up In Your Thinking* 45

Step 3-*Get Up In Your Words* 60

Step 4-*Get Up In Your Faith* 81

Step 5-*Get Up In Your Love* 95

Bibliography 114

Dedication

I would like to take this time to dedicate my first book to my two sons; Sidney Carter II and Sheldon Jeremiah Carter- The two of you gave me the inspiration and strength to complete this project; to my deceased mother Ruth Hazel Smith- I honor your legacy. Also to my Dad, Minister Clemmie Smith; thank you for your blessings, your love and your support. To my Husband, Ron Hart- Thank you for keeping things at the house going while I worked on my dream, this book. My theme scripture is Proverbs 4:23-"Above all else, guard your heart, for everything you do flows from it." (KJV)

Love Always,

Pamela

Acknowledgements

Acknowledgements: To all the other people who have helped me, there are so many names I may forget to mention some: To those who have researched, edited, planned, campaigned for support; to all those who have planted financial seeds to help publish this work and to all those who stood in the gap to pray; Thank you!

To my volunteer editorial staff: My sister, Greta Smith; my dad, Clemmie Smith; my two sons, Sidney and Sheldon Carter; Dr. Tymme Mitchell, Amy Butler, Lynn Abougi, Penny Rhodes, Tiff Williams, Starr Williams and Linda Fain.

A special shout out to DK Walker at En El Publishing for providing publishing services for my book and for encouraging me with "book publishing life coaching" that I needed to complete this project. He told me to finish strong and I DID!

I could not have done it without ALL of you! You are so awesome!

Forward by Dr. Karen Hollie-Psychotherapist & Life Coach Star L. Williams

Have you or someone you know, found yourself in a continual cycle of physical, emotional, mental or even spiritually abusive relationships? Pamela Hart, with her heart wide open, has written a poignantly transparent book sharing her personal 25 year story of abusive and victimizing relationships.

She recognized certain traits within herself that has caused her to continuously find herself in the victim's role. Ms. Hart writes about being able to heal from the abuse, how she got up again, and how she learned to walk in victory and freedom. Ms. Hart now shares her story in hopes that you, too, will be able to pick up yourself up and end the cycle of abuse and shame on your terms!

Ms. Hart describes exactly how she discovered toxic behaviors within herself that caused her to spin in the constant grip of abusive cyclical circumstances. The book describes her desire for a life of different and better, and in turn, how that desire lead her to first recognize characteristics including enabling, "people pleasing" for love, and co-dependence. She asserts that with the discovery of these traits came the realization of why she stayed in the grips of hurt, pain, and depression for decades. Pamela tells of learning the difference between sacrificing yourself for others in the Christian world and un-hanging yourself from self-inflicted situations.

If deep within, you find yourself being an enabler, codependent, or a "people pleaser" for love and acceptance, then you will easily relate to this book. If you have not yet discovered these traits within you, yet find yourself being constantly victimized in relationships, and wondering why, then this book will change your thought process. Joy and peace can be found. Happiness can be a part of your life. You Can Get Up Again!

If any of this resonates within your spirit, then this is the book for you. Pamela's experiences will show you how to walk out of victimization and into victory. Read. Heal. Live. Enjoy. Share.

Dr. Karen Holly-Thibodeaux
Author, Psychotherapist, Senior Pastor
Lifeway Church of Dallas

So many women live through situations that could be avoided if they had directions. This book introduces steps for them to understand how to take control instead of riding in the back seat of their own lives.

From the very beginning the introduction will grab the reader in the authenticity of Author Pamela Hart's life as she reveals her path of healing as this became the steps for others to follow. It takes commitment to own that responsibility and do something about what you don't like about your situation and to admit where you need to change.

5 Steps to Healing Your Heart is a great tool to coach women as they seek their own unique path to success. Step 2-Get Up In Your Thoughts- affirms that thinking different is a major step to becoming new and getting up.

You will be able to get up from disappointments, rejections, past and present hurts, self-doubt, and other emotional strongholds. This can be done with you being the person to do it and this very book that you are holding in your hands is the tool that will open the mind and heart of, not only women, but of any reader.

Starr L. Williams
Life Coach
Helping women discover their personal identity and future direction

Preface by Pamela Hart

5 steps to healing your heart- "You can get up again!"

I have written this book to help both women and men who suffer with painful and shameful relationships; including verbal and physical abuse If you are codependent, a people pleasure, an enabler, or a person who loves or gives too much of your heart, then this book is for you. I am here to support and encourage every woman who has had a difficult time setting relationship boundaries, especially those who have experience abuse or who have gone through traumatic relationships. This book provides 5 steps to promote the inner healing process needed to become a "survivor".

This book talks about the "Five steps" through my personal life events and through the use of spiritual principles of living.

If you have gone through personal life struggles, divorce, love break-ups, or a life breakdown, this book will HELP YOU! I am determined to do my part to educate both women and men on the facts about abuse and how it harms and can destroy a person's life, and one's family. Here are a few facts reported from the website called Domestic Violence statistics:

- Every 9 seconds in the US a woman is assaulted or beaten.
- Around the world, at least one in every three women has been beaten, coerced into sex or otherwise abused during her lifetime. Most often, the abuser is a member of her own family.
- Domestic violence is the leading cause of injury to women— more than car accidents, muggings, and rapes combined.

- Studies suggest that up to 10 million children witness some form of domestic violence annually.
- Nearly 1 in 5 teenage girls who have been in a relationship said a boyfriend threatened violence or self-harm if presented with a breakup.
- Every day in the US, more than three women are murdered by their husbands or boyfriends.
- Ninety-two percent of women surveyed listed reducing domestic violence and sexual assault as their top concern.
- Domestic violence victims lose nearly 8 million days of paid work per year in the US alone—the equivalent of 32,000 full-time jobs.
- Based on reports from 10 countries, between 55 percent and 95 percent of women who had been physically abused by their partners had never contacted non-governmental organizations, shelters, or the police for help.
- The costs of intimate partner violence in the US alone exceed $5.8 billion per year: $4.1 billion are for direct medical and health care services, while productivity losses account for nearly $1.8 billion.
- Men who as children witnessed their parents' domestic violence are twice as likely to abuse their own wives as sons of nonviolent parents.

Let me invite you to join me as I continue my recovery from abuse, emotional pain, suffering and shame and encourage you in your journey as well.

Have you ever been down and out, not knowing where to turn or what to do? Have you ever been so distressed over a relationship that you began to feel depressed or thought you would never get BACK UP?

Have you ever felt bullied in a relationship by someone you loved? Have you ever felt so ashamed of the secret issues going on behind closed doors that you wanted to scream? Have you ever wanted to tell someone, just ONE person, but knew you had to keep it a secret or else?

Well, I have!

One day I decided that I had to get up and heal my life. I looked myself in the mirror and saw that I was not the person I used to be. My life was out of control and I knew that no one else could do this for me. Getting up and healing one's life is hard work. But it is the most important thing you could ever do for your survival. I want you to get up and LIVE AGAIN! I want you to THRIVE, not just SURVIVE!

If I am speaking to your heart right now, you will feel it and you will know it. And you know it is time for you to make a change! Abuse hurts!

It does not matter what kind of abuse it is: physical abuse, verbal abuse, emotional abuse, financial abuse or mental abuse. It still hurts! Abuse hurts and creates wounds that can keep you stuck in misery and pain, feeling lost for years!

I don't want you to go through twenty five years of pain as I did before you are healed. As you read this book, there will be no judgements- no pressures.

Most of the time abuse occurs because the abuser is also suffering from a terrible heart injury from his childhood. That injured hurt person then continues to pass the hurt and pain on sometimes from generation to generation. I say it is time we all heal our hearts.

The truth is most people have experienced a broken heart. You are not alone.

MY HEART WAS BROKEN FOR A LONG TIME

My heart was broken for a long time. My brokenness came through abusive relationships with the men I chose to love. You see, I finally discovered after twenty five years of searching that I had a personality that included some traits such as: people pleaser, enabler and co-dependency. People pleasers are those who love to put other people before themselves. They will do for others first, take care of others first, yet the people pleaser will neglect themselves. The key is when we are people pleasers; we neglect ourselves and sacrifice to the point of pain and suffering just to "please" another person. We become an enabler when we keep make excuses for the person doing wrong acts; demonstrate bad behavior and we pretend they are ok. The enabler justifies the behavior of their loved one or the man in their life. This justification for bad behavior keeps the "One you love" acting out and then even blaming YOU for their bad behavior. They will say things like, "if you wouldn't talk so much, then I wouldn't have to get so upset" or "you make me act this way," or "You make me have to drink or do drugs," or "If you were doing what you were supposed to do, then this would not have happened".

When we keep being a people pleaser or an enabler, we show that we have a low self-esteem and a low self-image of ourselves. We become codependent when we show excessive emotional or psychological reliance on a partner who requires support due to an illness, emotional illness or any type of addiction. On the website for mental health America states, "Co-dependency is a learned behavior that can be passed down from one generation to another. It is an emotional and behavioral condition that affects an individual's ability to have a healthy, mutually satisfying relationship. It is also known as "relationship addiction" because people with co-dependency often form or maintain relationships that are one-sided, emotionally destructive and/or abusive. Co-dependent behavior is learned by watching and imitating other family members who display this type of behavior.

CO-DEPENDENCY IS A LEARNED BEHAVIOR

For example, a person who is codependent, usually unknowingly makes it easy for abusers, manipulators and controllers to be attracted to them. The abuse can be from people on your job, from people in your family, among friends but usually in a relationship; they are men who see how easy and willing you are to please them and they know exactly what to do to keep you pleasing them, enabling them to do things that keep you tied to them. Unfortunately, I have been a co-dependent in each of my marriages.

Today, I've learned how to set boundaries for myself and I continue to grow and learn how to control my own behavior. I have had to learn to not let what another does in a relationship-friendship or marriage keep me from being healthy. Personally, I have to choose to be mentally healthy every day.

If you decide to stay in a relationship with a person who is a narcissist, a controller, or someone with an addictive personality, then as a co-dependent person, you will have many difficult days ahead of you. Be determined to set boundaries because they are your lifeline and will help you stay mentally and even physically healthy.

So, what is the purpose of a boundary? Well, I am so glad you asked! A boundary is a space limit. It is your limit that you place over your physical space such as your personal things, limit for your personal space such as someone getting too close to you. We also have emotional limits, mental limits and spiritual space limits. The boundary you have set protects and takes care of YOU. Boundaries set the space between where you "end" and where the other person "begins". If you feel used, taken advantage of, or constantly treated poorly, then you may need to learn better boundary setting practices.

I believe most; if not all co-dependent women have an issue with setting boundaries. Men who are hitters, abusers, manipulators, or controllers whether knowingly or unknowingly seek women who are co-dependent. They will observe you and watch you over a period of time. These men will literally know you "better" than you know yourself. Women or men who are abusive will seek to control your "thoughts, actions and your feelings". They are toxic and they will eventually abuse you.

While searching for a way to heal my own heart, I discovered the truth about me! I tended to attract men with narcissistic, borderline, controlling, and addictive personalities. This was a shocking revelation for me.

Men with these personality disorders take advantage of women who are co-dependent. Co-dependent women overly please, excuse and justify their bad behavior. Co-dependent women become victims and find themselves in a toxic cycle. Narcissistic men and other men similar to this personality type, use women's desires of wanting to please them, love them and adore them as "The Weakness" that keep co-dependent women trapped in abusive relationships.

NOBODY TAUGHT YOU ABOUT BOUNDARIES

I want to tell you that IT IS NOT YOUR FAULT! No one ever trained you on how to have boundaries. No one told you about potential lovers who would turn out to be people who had narcissistic or borderline or even bipolar personality disorders. I never knew anything about "life's lessons on boundaries until I was about 40 years. By then, I had some major boundary issues.

It was only after studying and researching for 25 years, seeking knowledge, wisdom and understanding that God revealed to me that I was a woman who GAVE TOO MUCH OF MYSELF in love relationships to the men I attracted into my life!

When I entered into a love relationship, I would go all out to make things work out. Every time, I would end up being the enabler to their hurtful abuse, overly pleasing them and causing my own self destruction. I did not know how to say No! I was a nice person- too nice. I was a NICE church girl, easily forgiving their toxic behaviors. I overlooked their bad behaviors while taking their emotional beatings.

I found myself trapped, unable to free myself from the cycle of abuse. Needing them to love me, yet wanting them to stop abusing my love. This crazy cycle just continued from relationship to relationship. I needed to change "ME," before this crazy cycle would stop. I had to heal ME in order to STOP attracting the wrong kind of men into my life.

Today, I don't want to see women or men abused. I want both genders to be whole.

It took me 25 years to figure out this cycle and to begin healing my life through divine direction, knowledge and life changing strategies. I know how it feels to want to be healed, to want to be whole and at peace and not be able to get there. My hope is that you will find a place of pure love and acceptance on the pages of this book, a space to heal your broken heart. So don't give up, you can start your life over.

Today is "THE DAY" for you TO GET UP AGAIN. You CAN become free of toxic relationships. You CAN have healthy boundaries. You CAN LEAVE a life of being a victim. You CAN bring healing to your broken heart. I am proud of you and I am right here with you.

Now, take a deep breath and exhale. Things have already begun to get better. If you will commit to reading through these 5 steps and apply them to your life, you will forge a new path. You can start your healing journey today. Here is an agreement you can make between "You and You".

Sign up and start a new life today.

I, _____ will read All of the Five Steps so that I can change my Life and received my Transformation. Today's date is_____.

I have designed 5 steps to heal your heart and to help you get back up and to move forward.

1. Forgive UP 2. Think UP 3. Talk UP 4. Faith UP and 5. Love UP

As you apply these 5 steps, you will find the courage and strength to GET UP again and have the life you deserve!

Come join me as I continue my journey of healing and recovery. Just like me, you too can GET UP AGAIN and have the life you deserve.

INTRODUCTION: GET UP AGAIN

I grew up with 5 brothers and sisters in a middle class, African-American minister's home. We were blessed to have both parents. I felt very blessed because I saw kids at my school who lived with only one parent, usually their mother. Having both a mom and a dad added a sense of security to my life. As far as I was concerned, my world was perfect and I felt protected by both my mother and father. My father always had a job. He was into construction, building highways and bridges. He worked all week and then pastored for the church on Saturday and Sunday. My mother was a stay at home mom. She was quiet, yet a firm disciplinarian. All the kids knew not to mess with her. She could give you the "LOOK". She did not have to say many words to bring correction. Even when we were at a church service and we were acting up, talking or giggling, all she had to do was "give us that look." She was a woman with dignity; a strong black woman. She ran our home well. We knew that she was law, period! She cooked, cleaned and trained us to do the same. She and my dad where strict and determined to raise us up in the Lord.

I knew that I was different from most of the black girls in our town. I was what folks called a "PK", a preacher's kid. I was baptized when I was 10 years old. I loved going to church. I loved praising God. Even back then as early as age 13, people in the church would turn their heads and look back at me as I would say my "amen's and hallelujahs" as if I was in the wrong place. I loved to hear my father preach and I took notes at every sermon feverishly.

I lived in the small southern Texas town of Hillsboro, Texas. Hillsboro had a small school system. Growing up and being a Christian was challenging for me. Many kids when they are young, like to find someone to make fun of in school. I was the kid who was made fun of. I thought that some kids made fun of me for being a Christian. Today we would call it being bullied. Back then, it was just called "not being popular." There were kids who would say things like, "You live a life full of the DO NOT's".

"Don't curse, don't drink, don't do sex, don't skip school, don't do drugs, and don't have Fun."

For me, my life was perfect. I had 4 special girlfriends in my teen years: Angel, Joyce, Callie and Gwen, all black Christian girls. They were my church buddies. I just knew I would do life with them, no matter what! This was my world.

As I entered high school, I became excited about joining the tennis team. Playing on the tennis team became a status symbol to me. By being on the tennis team, I began to have Caucasian girlfriends. I had never realized what an opportunity this was until I began to receive all of the benefits of "tennis team Membership". My benefits included hanging out with white people, eating with white people, going places with white people and learning to talk like white people. This was a different world! My desire to have more of the "good life" exploded within me. Nevertheless, one day I learned that I was different from my "white girlfriends"; I was BLACK! I began feeling NOT GOOD ENOUGH again! Even though, we were considered a "good family," we were still considered a "black" family. I thought we were rich because I never lacked for anything and all my needs were met. That sense of protection would soon leave as I left home and entered college. Little did I know that I would not finish college, but that a great dark struggle would soon overtake me.

MY STRUGGLES, MY FAILURES, MY SHAME!

During my early adult years of struggle, I experienced two failed marriages, a secret abortion and spousal abuse (both physical and emotional). During my first marriage, I was unable to finish college due to marital conflicts. I began to battle depression, low self-confidence and low self-esteem. My life had become unmanageable and I began to seek personal help through reading books. Reading the Bible was my first choice. Later, I began to read all types of self-help books seeking to find someone who was going through my secret shame. Reading my Bible and self-help books kept me from totally falling apart.

I always loved talking to people and helping those who had broken hearts. During both high school and college many students and adults would talk to me about their problems. Years later as I became stronger on my journey to recovery, I knew I had to reach out to other women who were suffering in secret and in shame. I knew their pain; I could see it on their faces. When I looked at them, I was looking at myself. Helping other people, especially women who are still struggling with similar issues is the main motivating factor that drove me to write this book.

My search left me with questions of why I was still hurting. I wanted to learn what the missing piece in my life was. I was a single mom for some years and was raising my 2 sons. I had gone to college and earned a BAAS degree, earned an RN degree and even started working on my Masters. I had become a Licensed Minister, then worked as an Associate Pastor. After all of these changes to my life, I was still emotionally hurting and was still suffering with secret shame. Something was missing even though I was a Christian. I loved the Lord, but I had not received a revelation of the power and authority of being a believer. I was still experiencing the spirit of fear, doubt and confusion. I did not want to die without fulfilling my purpose on the earth. I knew I had not even touched it yet!

MAXIMIZE THE MOMENT

A few years passed me by and I stumbled upon the book "MAXIMIZE THE MOMENT" By Bishop T D Jakes. This book stirred my soul and increased the urgency within me for more revelation, more understand. This booked moved me greatly.

On page 232 of this book he asks, "Who will you spend your last drops with? And what cause have you dedicated your expenditures to? What noble commitment have you aligned yourself to, or are you just existing each day in a lethargic state of apathy and indifference? If you are, you are wasting your drops. You are losing the life's blood of your existence. What a sad malady to end your life and not knowing where you spent your last drops." I began to meditate back on the previous pages of his book; on page 230, Bishop Jakes writes, "Might I suggest that every encounter and accomplishment in life cost us something. No one attains anything without some type of expenditure. The reality is that all success, even failures, cause us to spend moments that will never be regained. When older people look at their loved ones and say, I'm tired, it is not the weariness of someone who needs sleep. It is the depleting of a spent life. They are experiencing the emptying out of the glass that started full of promise and potential."

After reading these words I thought deeply. My life was not the same. My soul had awakened. I knew I needed to change. I needed this "Maximized LIFE! But how? How could I even think about Maxing out when I felt powerless? There was a period of time where I just did a lot of thinking. I cried, I fasted, I prayed. I asked God to HELP ME! I asked the spirit to help me get up again.

Despite the many setbacks and adversities, I pressed my way to GETTING UP AGAIN and starting my life over.

In this season of my life, I write this book to motivate, empower, teach, and honor all women who have struggled to raise their children alone. I write this book to encourage those who have struggled to maintain their sanity while going through a divorce, abuse or depression. My spirit is here for women who have suffered abuse and women who have struggled with serious issues. I know that after reading this book, you will be able to get up again.

I am here to teach you 5 powerful steps in these chapters, that when applied to your daily life will give you freedom and peace. Come with me as we share these steps to getting up. Are you ready?

GET UP IN YOUR FORGIVENESS

Step One *-Get Up in Forgiveness-*

I would love to tell you that forgiveness is easy, but sorry, I can't. It won't be easy, but it will be worth it. Forgiveness is one of the spiritual laws of the universe. A spiritual law is something that works the same for everyone. It is consistent. A law will work the same for you as it does for me. That means it will work every time. The first step in healing your heart in order to get up and start life over is forgiveness. But, you need to understand the law of forgiveness in order to operate this principle for maximum benefits.

Choosing to forgive has been a major player for me during my healing journey of abuse. Operating in the law of forgiveness is crucial to healing and transformation. Transformation, changing from the inside out is really what we all must do in order to have REAL AUTHENTIC healing.

One day, I decided to forgive the men that had been a part of my life so that I could be free from all bitterness and emotional pain. Did you know that unforgiveness will kill you? There was no need for me to allow the poison of unforgiveness to ruin the rest of my life. You can forgive and move on at the same time. Forgiving all the men or people that have hurt you will give you an inner cleansing and a freedom like you've never experienced. You will feel so exuberant, so clean, and so peaceful.

Many people, especially women are under extreme stress. Women get so busy taking care of family and friends, not really focusing on their own bodies much less on their soul and spirit. What I decided to do for my recovery is called "extreme self-care"! Believe me, if you have suffered any form of abuse, then you need to take some time to dedicate yourself to doing some "extreme self-care." What is extreme self-care? It is the process of learning to love yourself as you are.

EXTREME SELF-CARE IS THE ACT OF TAKING GOOD CARE OF YOURSELF

Extreme self-care is the act of taking very good care of yourself through various methods that promote your overall health and well-being. It includes: Resting, sleeping, getting massages, exercising, eating healthy food, drinking pure water, taking nutritional supplements that help with stress such as B-Vitamins and other herbal supplements that may be helpful as well. Other methods of self-care include going to see movies that make you laugh, going on trips that bring you joy, connecting with new friends and seeing family members that you have not seen in a long time. You will begin to come alive again as you take these steps that will start your healing process. Take care of you first. When flying in an airplane, we are always instructed to "put the oxygen on your face first, then assist someone else. Is this selfish you might ask? Well, yes! The good kind of selfishness. You must learn to love yourself before you can truly love someone else. The bible even says, "Love your neighbor as you love yourself. This means: Just like you love yourself is the way you will love other people. So, if you do not love yourself well, you will not love other people well. Life coach Cheryl Richardson in her book called Take time for your life wrote on page 37 of her book; "It's easy to ignore our emotional and physical health until there's a problem. Most of us wait until it's too late. We lead busy, hectic lives, putting work or the needs of others before our own self- care. We fill our bodies with fast food, tolerate high levels of stress, and run non-stop on adrenaline. Like the Energizer bunny, the body keeps going and going-then one day, something goes wrong. We get sick, hear the diagnosis of an unexpected illness, or notice that we just can't seem to get things done the way we use to. That's when most people, like my client Jonah, finally start paying attention to their health". As we start this journey, we cannot help but think of all of our "other women friends who could use a little help too! Life coach Cheryl Richardson also said in her book called Take care of yourself on page 160, "In the spirit of extreme self-care, pamper and care for your body on a regular basis. Schedule a massage or some other form of bodywork to help your body relax and rejuvenate. In the past, getting a massage was considered either a luxury or a necessary treatment for injury. Today, with our increased levels of stress and sedentary (but frantic!) lifestyles, our bodies hold far more tension and anxiety. This has made massage and other forms of bodywork (like reiki and reflexology) important ways to fuel our bodies. Bodywork restores balance, gets the circulation flowing, and increase your energy." She future states, "Bodywork is no longer a luxury, it's a standard. Book a treatment today"!

I began to think of some of my women friends whom I know still have great bitterness towards some of the men in their lives. If someone says something to them about male and female relationships, they go off on a tangent. Just listening to them complain about "how terrible all these men are" lets me know that there is still some unforgiveness floating around in their hearts. We, both women and men, sometimes forget that we must stop and take some quality time for our own bodies and minds to rest, to heal and to FORGIVE. Decide to start this journey of healing now. YOU CAN GET UP AGAIN.

FORGIVE BY ALIGNING YOUR THOUGHTS

I have come to shake you up before it's too late. Wake up and allow the healing that comes through forgiveness to penetrate your soul. This healing starts with your thoughts. Your thinking is way more powerful than you may have ever imagined. After we align our thoughts, we then must align our mouths. (See chapter 2). It is important to give verbal affirmation to our hopes, dreams and aspirations. Start saying phrases like, "I am willing to forgive him," or "I am willing to forgive her." Let me tell you, how you think about forgiveness is the key to letting go of old hurts. Yes, with our thoughts we can think forgiveness. Yes, with our mouths we can say, "I forgive you". You see, Life and Death are in the power of the tongue. Your tongue is very powerful. Go ahead and try it out. Place a name of someone that you choose to forgive today! In the blank space write their name. I choose to forgive_____. You can fill in the blank with the person's name, situation or the hurt you are carrying deep in your heart.

THE POWER OF FORGIVENESS

There is power in forgiveness. Forgiveness can break chains. There is a chorus of a song that goes like this, "Breaks every chain, breaks every chain, breaks every chain". It breaks the chain of emotional suffering. It breaks the chain of bitterness. It breaks the chain of hate. Forgiveness breaks the chain of shame. The power of Life or Death is in your tongue. You, through the power of forgiveness, can choose life over death, freedom over prison. When we choose not to forgive, we choose emotional and mental imprisonment. By forgiving, we choose to move forward with our lives. The way you live in your future, depends on how well you FORGIVE Today. Choose life. Choose life for yourself, Choose life for your children, and choose life for your destiny and life for your legacy that you will leave behind in the earth. There are people waiting for your "Yes" to forgiveness.

Here's an idea I would like to share with you. Write a forgiveness letter. Write a letter stating why you feel the way you feel. It is amazing what can happen when you write this type of letter. Action that is in alignment with your thoughts and words is very, very powerful. This type of action shows the universe that you are ready to "Let It Go and Let God handle it".

I became driven to learn about the Law of forgiveness. One method that will help you to begin to practice this "first step" is to think about who you need to offer an apology. I decided to embrace the concept of apologizing even when others would not apologize to me. You may want others who have offended you to ask for forgiveness, but many times people will just not do it. It could be pride, ego or embarrassment; whatever the case, do not let that stop you from doing what is right and what will free you so that you can move forward in your life. Just so you know, family and friends are not always so forgiving. Nor will many of your family or friends give you the apology you may seek. That is why you must decide to forgive regardless of what others do or don't do. You see, I have had to walk the road of forgiveness toward others many times even when some of my friends no longer wanted to have me as their friend. This hurts, but you will survive if you choose to walk in forgiveness anyway. Regardless of rather the other person forgives you or apologizes to you, rise to the occasion and walk in forgiveness. Just remember that your desire for reconciliation may not be accepted. They simply may not be ready for that step.

THE PROCESS OF FORGIVENESS

Here are five steps of forgiveness that helped me walk in forgiveness.

The first step is 1. Admit that you have been hurt by someone or admit that someone has offended you. 2. Let yourself feel the emotions of that hurt and identify what that feeling is for you. 3. Cancel the Debt towards that person-Write down the offense or insult that the person or persons have done toward you. 4. Set your limits with the person who hurt you. 5. Make a decision to forgive and keep moving forwards. Remember forgiveness is a decision, not a feeling.

The healing power of forgiveness is essential in allowing us to move forward even after our spirit, soul or body has been wounded. Especially after an event such as a divorce, physical or emotional abuse, or broken friendships. Without the desire to move forward and let go, many may stay stuck in unforgiveness.

Unforgiveness leads to bitterness. Unforgiveness can cause a physical breakdown in the body that can lead to arthritis, high blood pressure, heart disease, headaches and a number of other illnesses. Unforgiveness can also lead to emotional breakdowns, both minor and major mental dysfunctions and mental disease.

FORGIVENESS IS A DECISION

Forgiveness is a decision and a desire to forgive another person with an act of compassion. This compassion will give you the ability to release the desire to punish someone for an offense. Forgiveness does not refer to the offense, but to the wound that was caused by the offense. It is a form of turning the other cheek as Jesus said in the New Testament scriptures. These scriptures also speak of forgiving the same person numerous times. The scriptures says to forgive 70 times 7. What the scriptures are saying is, "stop counting," and don't get stuck on how many times the person offends you. But, refuse to react with revenge. Forgiveness is releasing the anger, pain and suffering from the offense. Revenge is the act of getting even or hurting that person who did you wrong. However, revenge reduces you to your worst self and puts you on the same level as the offender.

Key Points to ponder:

1. Forgiveness does not make light of the wrong the person has done against you.

2. Forgiveness does not deny the horrible situation that happened to you or accept that the wrong is ok.

3. Forgiveness does not alleviate the consequences the offender must face or receive from the behavior or actions they committed.

4. The offender must realize that even though the person chooses to forgive the offender, forgiveness is a process. The feeling of forgiveness takes time. It is a process and it is not always easy. So don't be hard on yourself if your feelings do not change immediately.

5. Forgiveness is a strength, not a weakness. Forgiving another person is one of the most powerful things another person can do for an offender. Refusing to forgive will give power to the person who has hurt you and allows the situation that was hurtful to continue hurting you.

6. Forgiveness does not mean you must forget what was done to you. You are human and you have a brain and you have memory. You can forgive, but you may never forget. Forgiveness does not mean that you forget.

One very strong point I want to make about unforgiveness is it will hurt you more not to forgive,

than to forgive. It will also hurt you more if you choose not to forgive the offender. A law means that it works every time. There is no discrimination in a law. The law of forgiveness will work every time if you work the process. It works for females as well as males. It works for the rich as well as for the poor; in other words, it works for everyone. The power in forgiveness comes by personal application. How are you using this power to transform your life? You can use it in your marriage, with your children, on your job, in your church or in your personal relationships. Here are some examples in my personal life where I had to choose forgiveness if I wanted to move forward with my life.

MY FIRST HUSBAND AND FORGIVENESS

My first husband and I separated in the 80s while living in Kansas (let's call him Bob, Nope...Let's call him Tyrone! yea, that feels better!). We went through a divorce after an eight year marriage. We remained in the same little town in the state of Kansas. We agreed on personal items and on transportation vehicles. At that time I was working as an LVN on the 11-7 shift and taking college classes during the day. When I got off work this particular morning, I could not find my car. I thought someone had stolen it. I kept looking and walking around in the parking lot. I felt I was going crazy. Finally, I saw it! There it was! It was unbelievable! It was his beaten up old car. I could not believe it was there at "MY" job. I went up to the old worn out car and I saw a note under the windshield wipers. It stated, "Here's my car for you to keep. I need your car because it is newer. I am taking a trip to Arizona for the weekend. Please don't call the police. I promise I will be back within 7 days and you can have your car back." Well, to say the least, I was livid. I thought only angry thoughts. I cried as I found the key to his car where the note instructed me to find it. I thought to myself, "Who would do such a thing?" I called my mom and dad. I told them how angry I was. They offered me suggestions, but nothing could calm my nerves or heal my broken heart of betrayal. Yes, that was one day that I felt betrayed. Nevertheless, I made it through that day and I made it through that week.

BEING A VICTIM AND STAYING IN THE SUFFERING

As I reflect back on that day, I realize that I did not see it coming. I was not focused. I was feeling sorry for myself and into "suffering." I did not know this at the time that a person could be into, "SUFFERING" (SUFFERING IS WHEN YOU FEEL LIKE A VICTIM AND YOU DON'T HAVE THE TOOLS OR STRATEGIES TO GET OUT OF THE PATTERN OF SUFFERING OR OF OTHER PEOPLE ALWAYS DOING YOU WRONG). This situation where he took my car was totally unexpected. I was angry, and I could only focus on what he had done to me. I did not know anything about the law of attraction and my role in my pain. Yes, I had a role in this pain and suffering. It would take years before I would discover that I had played a vital role in this nightmare. So, I continued to feel used and abused. I had not discovered who I really was. I had no authority of power, nor a belief in abundance and no boundaries in my life.

After he returned, I said few words to him. He did return my keys. I continued to file for divorce. Years later he called me while I was pregnant with my second son to ask for forgiveness. He had called my father's home and asked one of my sisters if he could get my number to make amends with me. After I gave her permission to give him my number, he called me.

I spoke with him briefly and he asked for forgiveness for all of the physical and emotional abuse that happened in the marriage. As I listened to him, my mind raced back to my stored long term memory department. It seemed as though he was talking about another person. I began to recall several areas of pain and abuse as he spoke.

My mental list looks like this:

1. The time he pushed me out of the car onto the ground while he was on the driver's side, and I was sitting on the passenger's side. While

we were talking, he became angry at me for disagreeing with him. After he pushed me out of the car, he drove off with me lying on the ground. He did not even look back. I was so embarrassed and humiliated. I remember looking around to see if anyone was watching; however, I didn't spot anyone.

2. Spitting in my face and calling my mother a "Bitch" in the parking lot of a restaurant before going inside. **("YES, I think he is still living and NO, I didn't put a hit out on his life.")**

On this particular day, we had gotten out of our car to go inside of the restaurant to meet his pastor friend who just happened to be the Pastor of a Methodist Church. He was a very caring man who had shown kindness to me several times when he had noticed my first husband, "Tyrone" treating me badly. He gently suggested to my ex-husband "Tyrone" while we were ordering food that I could order a "whole entire meal for myself" instead of sharing one with him. My ex-husband rarely let us order separate meals. It was his rule that we share "one" meal and save money. His Methodist Pastor said, "Let her order what she wants; I will pay for her order." My heart had been beating so fast, as the words wanted to erupt out of my mouth to tell the Pastor how he had just treated me in the parking lot, but I was too afraid! I knew I would have to go home to an even angrier man if he found out that I told. So, I chose to "be quiet" and enjoy MY entire meal. The meal that had been purchased just for ME!

Now, back to the phone call: As I listen to "Tyrone" apologize, he never mentioned the specifics of what he had really done to me and he never really acknowledged the pain and suffering that I had experienced in that marriage! I now understood that he could only do the best that he could based on his own past hurts, addictions or lack of self-esteem. I suddenly realized that I was no longer the person he was TALKING ABOUT anymore! And it did not really matter much anymore. However, I was glad that he had called and that he had a desire to make peace with me and WITH HIMSELF! And with HIS GOD!

FEAR CAN KEEP YOU STUCK

I NOW know that FEAR had kept me stuck in that situation for a long time. And I was no longer in FEAR. I was no longer his wife. I told him that I had forgiven him a long time ago and that ALL was well between us. I still had some fading memories, but I praised God silently on the phone that night that the emotional pain was gone, or ALMOST gone.

I have never heard from him again since that night on the telephone, but I rest peacefully knowing that my heart is free from the mental and emotional pain that was caused in that marriage. I am thankful that I was able to forgive him, release him and let him go.

Through divorce, I was able to protect myself from letting this person hurt me again. I do not advocate divorce but unfortunately, in cases of unresolved physical, emotional, and psychological abuse, it is necessary. My main personal Transformation was "ME, myself, and I." I began to ask the God of the universe why I had allowed another human being to treat me so badly. I was totally naive to Kingdom thinking and Kingdom principles of living. I was totally unaware of how to create what I wanted. I did realize that I suffered from low self-esteem and low self-confidence. I did not believe in myself and I felt so beaten down. I did not know how to pray the word of God, or understand how to live by faith. I did not understand that FAITH was a lifestyle. I needed a spiritual teacher and leader who could help me find an enlightened path. Someone who had gone through the valley and who knew God could still work a miracle today.

I needed a community of faith believing, word teaching people to hang around with so that I could experience the presence of God. I did love my first husband, but I did NOT understand how to set boundaries for myself or understand self-love.

I ALLOWED him to abuse me. The author, Sheila Wray Gregoire in one of her Blogging articles on To honor, to Love and Vacuum on Feb 26, 2015 states about someone who is being verbally abusive, " So he is being verbally abusive, and they are trying to deal with it by loving on him. If we're loving and kind, he will change, right? Nope. Being nicer to someone who is mean encourages them to do it more. They feed off of that. Many marriage problems need you to be nicer and more giving, but many do not. In this case, what this woman needs to do is stand up to her husband and say "I see that you are angry, and I'd be happy to talk to you when you're calmed down. But I will not stay in a room with you while you say horrible things to me-and then get up and leave."

FORGIVE US OUR DEBTS AS WE FORGIVE OTHERS

The Lord's Prayer says, "Forgive us our debts as we also have forgiven our debtors." This biblical excerpt tells us that we are to ask God for forgiveness and also that we desire forgiveness for our trespasses, and mistakes as well.

The dictionary says that forgiveness is renunciation or cessation of resentment, indignation or anger as a result of a perceived offence, disagreement, or mistake. This means that you stop being resentful, YOU stop being angry and you let go of the perceived offence. This means that you no longer hold the mistake or disagreement against the person. When we ask God to forgive US, don't we long for him to release us from our mistakes and offences? In the same way God forgives all of us for our trespasses, and we should treat other people with forgiveness and let go of our resentment and release them from their mistakes and offences. There is a popular song in the Christian community that just came to my mind. It says two powerful words…"I'm forgiven." this entire song is about being forgiven by God for stuff you thought God would never forgive you for.

But, God loves us and has given us his son Jesus, that whosoever believes in him should not perish, but have everlasting life. "You are forgiven."

Forgiveness is essential in overcoming those hurts that seem impossible. Forgiveness has a place for everyone, regardless of age or level of hurt.

Many in our new generation do not know how to start the process of true forgiveness. As I look around, I can see the old law of dealing with any offence in the old testament in operation today such as: "an eye for an eye and a tooth for a tooth." This belief has been going strong for over 2000 years, that many still practice it today. This practice went like this: if you did something to me, I will do the same to you. It meant: if you hurt me, I will hurt you back.

Today, there is a lot of hurt in the world. People are out of work. Families are struggling to keep everything going, and many of our families just give up. Our Institutions of religion, whether Jewish or Christian seem to have failed to communicate how to forgive each other.

Here are 5 steps in the forgiveness process that helped ME to forgive others.

1. Admit that you have been hurt by someone; such as an offense, or hurt by an insulting situation. Admitting you are hurt does not mean you don't act like what the person did to you was not that bad. Don't start blaming yourself for not being a better person. Start journaling about the hurt and the pain you feel. This will help you work through the anger and the hurt.

2. Let yourself feel the emotions and identify what that feeling is for

you. You may have feelings of regret and anger from the offense. These feelings are a normal response to an offense or an insult.

3. Cancel the Debt towards that person-Write down the offense or insult that the person or persons have done toward you. Then write out the words "Write paid in full or debt cancelled" with the person name in bold print. Usually this letter is just for yourself to keep. Also you may burn the letter as an act of "burning the debt letting it all go up in the smoke."

4. Set Your Limits with the person who hurt you. You need what is called boundaries. It means you forgive, but you realized the person may have not changed and may never change, so you will put up safeguards for yourself. These safeguards or boundaries help protect you from associating with that person, or a boundary can allow you to tell that person you will no longer accept the treatment. You can decide not to talk with the person if they began to insult you or walk away. Don't continue to desire approval from someone who has insulted you, or who has hurt you.

5. Make a decision to forgive. Remember forgiveness is a decision. It is a choice, not a feeling. Do not use what the person has done to you as a weapon to make them feel guilty or to hold it over their heads. Release them and let the person go.

If you have made a decision to forgive a person, I want to congratulate you for this massive move to forgive the person for the pain you feel from the insult. If you are struggling with this issue of forgiveness, you are not alone. Let me tell you that most likely the person who hurt you is not thinking about all of the pain they caused you. The pain caused by the person's insensitivity or offense has hurt you more than it hurt the person who wronged you. I encourage you to continue this FIRST STEP of getting back up again and healing your heart as you apply these stages of forgiveness. When applied, you will move forward with your life and find the joy, peace and healing that you deserve!

Now, I want to discuss "Self-Forgiveness." You see, many of us will strive to forgive those who have hurt us, but we may struggle even more with forgiving ourselves. I use to struggle with forgiving myself with the many bad decisions that I had made. One of those decisions was the one to have an abortion.

Honestly, all of my life I had been on the side of "Pro-Life". I could not imagine being anything else nor could I believe that one day I would have to make a decision to keep my baby or to end the life of my child.

One day after my first divorce, I became involved with someone. We were both Christians and we were intellectually committed to wait for sex until after marriage. I did not even know at that time if I really wanted to marry him. As the relationship continued and I having been use to a married life, allowed myself to become involved with my lover in an intimate way. I was ashamed of myself because I so much wanted to live by the word of God as I understood it. We both were members of a Baptist church at that time and he was in the ministry.

FOR THE FIRST TIME I CONSIDERED ABORTION

After becoming ill and going to my doctor's appointment, I found out that I had only one good working kidney and also my other kidney was located in my abdomen area called a pelvic kidney that I knew nothing about. The doctor's said it was something that I was born with, but my other doctors had no reason to ever discover it. My Gynecologist said he had little experience with this situation and he felt I would have a difficult pregnancy. My doctor said that I could end up on a Kidney dialysis with this type of pregnancy. I left the appointment very confused and scared. For the first time, I considered abortion because I was scared to face these medical issues and I would also have to deal with being pregnant and not married. I did not want to face the possibility of being on a kidney machine, going through a difficult pregnancy, or risk my life for this child that I did not even know yet. I was not considering that the child was already alive and deserved to live. I was NOT considering God's will for the life of my child. I did not have the faith to overcome this great dark struggle. My feet began to swell and I became weak: weak physically, weak emotionally, weak spiritually, weak in my faith in God. I told my parents and they came to visit me. My mother and father were in the ministry, yet they never once verbally or openly judged me, nor criticized me for my pregnancy or confusion. They suggested to me that I should come home for a while. I went home for about a week to Texas, but after receiving calls from the baby's daddy, I decided to go back to the state where we both were living. I returned to college. I returned to going back to the Baptist church I was attending. But, I was still confused. All I knew was: I did not want to take a chance with my health and risk being sick over this, I did not know if I wanted to get married just because of this.

THAT NEWS LEFT ME WITH GREATER PRESSURE!

The pressure in my Mind continued. I had an inner war going on! Little did I know that a year from that time that I would marry this baby's daddy. However, at that time being with the baby's daddy still left me unsure of what I wanted to do. The baby's daddy, my second husband, (let's call him Peter) wanted me to marry him and keep the baby. Since he was an older man in his later years of life, he told me that he may never have another chance to have a child at that time in his life. He told me that the doctors said that his sperm count was so low that it would take a miracle for him to produce a child. That news left me with greater pressure. I was still scared! I still felt ashamed! I was still facing the medical issue that could leave me sick! I did not want to take that chance! It had only been a year that I had recently divorced after being married for 9 years to a man who was abusive to me. I was not sure about making a lifetime commitment to another man whom I had become emotionally and sexually involved.

WAIT, I CHANGE MY MIND!

Filled with confusion, stress and anxiety, I ran off alone to another state and had the abortion. I remember laying on the cold table, feeling ashamed and scared, I suddenly yelled out right in the middle of the procedure, **"wait, I change my mind."** The Doctor and Nurses were both shocked as they all said, "sorry, it is too late, we have already started to suction." I felt so lethargic and depressed that I began to cry aloud. The doctor said that he wanted to meet with me in his office afterwards. He told me that he thought I had made up my mind and that if he knew I was still unsure, then he would not have done the abortion. I sat there and continued to cry in his office. He said he could tell that I was different than anyone else he had cared for in his office. He told me that he was so sorry and that he wished I would have talked with him. He was also an OB/GYN doctor who took women to their full term and delivered babies in the other side of his practice. Today, I hold on to the hope that the encounter he had with me and my abortion "Changed his mind" how he did abortions in his clinic or maybe he stopped doing abortions altogether. I may never know. I do not even know his name or the name of the clinic. I chose to forget.

With a weak body and mind, I left out of his office and struggled to get into my car. I could not believe that it was over so quickly. "This was my child I had done away with." I thought to myself. I tried to drive home. I pulled over on the side of the highway. I lay in the front seat crying and mourning my loss. I felt that I did not want to live. I cannot believe that I had killed my child," I thought over and over again. There was nothing I could do. As I made it home, I felt like anyone who looked at me must have known what I had done. I felt so ashamed and wondered could God ever forgive me.

IT SHOULD HAVE BEEN JUST AN ORDINARY DAY

It should have been just an ordinary day. However, this day had turned into a life changing decision. I had made a destiny decision. I would never know this child on planet earth. By the next year I had decided to marry the baby's father. I began to increase in faith for a child. My second husband reminded me what his doctor had said: His sperm count was too low and it would take a miracle to impregnate someone. I began to believe in Miracles. I believed that I was forgiven and I asked God to help me to get pregnant. I began to change my thinking: Saying, "He did it for Sarah, Abraham's wife when her womb was barren. He did it for Mary, Jesus's mother and she never had sex with a man. He did it for Elizabeth who gave birth to John the Baptist in her old age." I began to believe that My God could do it for us too.

It was in 1990 that I began to believe God for a Miracle! I desired to have a son! It was in 1992 that the Lord blessed me with a handsome, beautiful baby boy. Then a second miracle occurred in 1996, a second handsome and beautiful son was born for me to spoil. I felt that the Lord has given me favor. T.D. Jakes said that "FAVOR AINT FAIR". Well, he was right! I had all three-MERCY, GRACE AND FAVOR!

My first King was Sidney and my second King was Sheldon. They were the sons I thought I would never have. Some years later, I would think about the aborted child. I would imagine that the aborted child was a baby girl and she would have been my first born. I wondered what she would have looked like. Wondering how she could have changed the world. I thought about all the blessings we missed from her not being here in our lives and how differently our lives may have been if this baby girl had lived. I still would wonder from time to time if God would ever forgive me. I "realized" that I still carried the shame of the abortion. Unfortunately, it took me about 10 years to know within my heart that I was forgiven. I forgave myself and I now know the "forgiveness of God". Nevertheless, it would take NINETEEN years before I could speak of this loss publicly in one of my sermons. I thank God for releasing my voice in an arena where many Christian girls and women suffer alone with secret shame and secret hurt. This type of private pain and loss have been the reason for suicides, depression, and other psychological disorders. There is no real accurate statistics of how many women really suffer from this loss since many never tell of their abortions or discuss the psychological trauma they have experienced.

HE IS JUST THAT FORGIVING!

Now, let us examine God's forgiveness. I have personally experienced the love of God in my own life. The scriptures says for God so loved the world that he gave his only begotten son and if we believe in who he is, then we would have eternal life, the blessed life; a life lived in fullness of purpose. Knowing that God loves you and that the God of the universe has the power, ability to wipe your slate clean is a life changing concept. It does not matter what you have done, you can start over again, get up again and live an empowered life.

ASK FATHER GOD TO COME INTO YOUR HEART!

Accepting God's forgiveness is crucial. All you have to do is, ASK father God to come into your heart and ask him to let his presence into your heart. The God who created the universe will step right into your car, (even after an abortion), your bathroom, or your bedroom and most of all- your heart. He is just that powerful, loving and kind. He has that much GRACE. He is just that FORGIVING.

GET UP IN YOUR THINKING

Step Two *-Get UP in your Thinking-*

You can get up again, even in your thinking. This is step 2. It is called the Law of Thinking. This law literally transformed my life to a whole new person. Every problem in your life is a wisdom problem. Wisdom is learning how to think through a set of problems and then knowing how to apply knowledge to the problems in your life. Wisdom is the use of applied knowledge at its best. What we don't know can hurt us. People perish, people give up, people can be destroyed and lose out on life because they lack knowledge and understanding. I want you to know that if you have had struggles, heartache and pain; you are reading the right book. You see, your life failures can be lessons to help others get up again. The things that have hurt you can be turned into victories to help others. Your life can be used as a stepping stone to help you, your family, your friends and even people you may never meet. Your life failures can be used to help others rethink their choices which will affect their destiny. It has been said that the devil is our enemy and he gets into our thoughts and tells us that we cannot make it. It is said that the devil tells a single parent, you will never be able to raise these kids. The devil has been accused of telling a father who just lost that job that he is a failure and that he will not be able to even feed his children. But the devil is a liar. And just in case you don't even believe in a devil, then we ourselves through our own doubt and unbelief in our ability to be successful, will think negative thoughts about our past, our present and our future that will keep us stuck in life.

SOMETIMES, WE ARE OUR WORST ENEMIES

Sometimes, we are our own worst enemy. Even if you have so much mess in your life that you believed in your mind that you could never be on top; I am here to tell you that God has so much more mercy that he will help you find your way out of that mess. Even if you feel that you are guilty of the worst of wrongs, then I am here to tell you that God offers you great grace and favor. Now, if you tell me, "but I have so much drama in my life;" I would tell you," God delivers drama queens and even drama kings." Let me share with you a powerful awakening truth. You are what you think about all day. You create your world through your thoughts. Nothing just happens. Nothing just happens to you. Nothing just happens to me. Your reality, your world is not created in just a few thoughts, but it is the compilation of your feelings, your fears, your faith, your hope, your worries and the power of you thinking.

Let me encourage you to learn how to take time to think. I want to encourage you to learn how to meditate. Meditating on good things, positive things for a while will help create the right environment for you to activate the law of thinking. This activation will create a mindset. What you think or meditate upon is your mindset and your belief system. When we put a consistent group of thoughts out into our world we will attract those vibrations back to us. I remember my mother always quoting a verse in the bible that said, "Do unto others as you would have others do unto you." She was teaching her children that if we treated people good, then good would come our way. But if we treated people badly, then bad things would come our way.

My mother had never heard of the law of attraction or the law of thinking, but she knew what the bible said: ("that as a man thinks in his heart, so is he"). My father and my mother knew biblical principles worked. Let me share with you this concept: Thoughts are things. Whatever you meditate on for a long time, will eventually manifest or you will act on some aspects of what you have been meditating on. We create our reality and our world with our thoughts. All that is happening in your world is a response to the thoughts and the patterns of thoughts you are offering to the world, the universe.

Your thinking patterns are also known as vibrational thoughts. When vibrational thoughts are consistently maintained, those vibrations will attract some type of manifestation. Your manifestation will depend on this major factor: Do you want to produce something or manifest something? If you're thinking and what you say out of your mouth can match your faith level or belief level in your heart; then you will have a manifestation. Have you heard the saying that goes: "believe and receive, doubt and do without? Well, it is so true.

The word of God says to have the faith of God or the God kind of faith. Many times we just did not understand what our thinking had to do with God's faith. God's thoughts are higher than our thoughts; therefore, our job on planet earth is to raise up our vibrations to meet God's vibrations. To raise up our thoughts to meet God thoughts. This is what is meant by statements like, "seek his face", "be still and know that I am God"," I am that I am, and "think on these things." When we stay in faith, or as some teachers call it; staying in the vortex, (Abraham/Esther Hicks), we will stay in the presence of God. And when we are in the vortex, in faith or other words, in his presence; good things will happen, miracles will happen, a woman gets pregnant and 2 miraculous children are born! My miracle, your miracle will happen.

We call it miracles. Thinking and believing are tools God has given us to change our life.

Let me remind you that step one of healing your heart was walking in forgiveness. Now we are on step two.

LEARNING HOW TO MEDITATE IS VERY NECCESSARY

This step two, learning how to think and meditate is a very necessary step in your life in having the life you deserve. Do you want to be happy, peaceful, empowered and successful, then learn how to think and meditate? You will make your way prosperous. I believe God wanted all humans to be prosperous when he created us in the earth realm.

See, we were meant to live in "Paradise," to live a garden filled life. A life in Eden. A life of ease and rest! Yes, we were created to live a life of ease and rest. I know this may sound pretty unbelievable or even a bit like hogwash to you. But it is true. When God created man, he put them in a beautiful home and gave them everything they would need to live a prosperous and successful life. Adam and Eve messed this up with their thinking and lack of belief. They chose to LISTEN to a contradicting voice. Wow! This is still true today. God will walk with us and keep us in peace and rest as we meditate on him and his word.

We will walk in our purpose on this earth. We will fulfill our destiny. Are you ready to SUPERSIZE your thoughts and dreams? I am! You are a divine creator of your own reality. God has given you the power in your Mind, through your thought life, you can began to change your world.

When we change our thinking and realize that our mind holds the key to the greatest life we could ever have on earth, positive manifestation occurs. This truth has been what some teachers and prophets called "The Secret." It has only been a secret because we would NOT believe how powerful we are and that we were made in God's image and likeness. When we know who we really are, we will change our thoughts to God thoughts and began to create a new life filled everyday with love, joy, peace and goodwill toward all humanity. Your life right now, which is your manifestation is the sum total of your thinking. This is Revelation!

In this step two process to getting up again and living a powerful life, you hold the key. What do you want in your life? You can have what you want if you will commit to holding the vibrational thought long enough until that level of manifestations occur. A life is built thought upon thought, line upon line, and precept upon precept. If you can think it and believe it in your mind, or if you can get there in your mind, you can manifest it in your world.

Do you want a beautiful, gigantic house on the hill in a richly suburban neighborhood nestled behind tall pine trees with a large swimming pool, your very own tennis court, and don't forget the beautiful spa with the heated hot tub? Yes, well you can have all of this. And what about a life filled with love in your heart and surrounded by family and friends who love you unconditionally? Do you long for this? Just put your order into the universe and go to work thinking. If you have never thought this way, all of this can sound like magical thinking or in other words, Hogwash!

Many people think negatively on a daily basis. People can really be in some bad situations. As a RN who have worked in a Forensic Psychiatric hospital, I have read some horrific stories that would blow you away. Some people are just in some bad situations. In my many therapeutic RN sessions and coaching sessions with people, they describe themselves as feeling like they are living in hell. And how can anyone get out of hell? How can anyone get pulled out of hell, swim out of hell or even walk out of hell? OUR THINKING MUST CHANGE IF WE WANT TO GET OUT OF A HELLISH SITUATION.

What we call life CAN sometimes feel like being stuck in the miry clay. Well, I really don't know what miry clay is, but it sounds like I have been in it a couple of times. I have read about the muck and the miry clay in the bible and anyone who was in it, struggled to get out of it. They had to want to get out of it. That is it! You have to have a desire to want to get unstuck in your thinking. But first, there must be a realization that you are stuck and going nowhere in your life. Remember, your thoughts make up your life.

Just writing about this is so exciting and so refreshing. I hope you can feel the energy now and the increase in your vibrations. Go right ahead and tune your frequency to the right station so you can hear me loud and clear. You can get up in your thinking, you can change your thoughts to new positive thoughts! CAN YOU HEAR ME NOW?

I want to ask you another question. May I call upon a deeper part of your mind, your heart? Your heart is your innermost being and it is THE PLACE where you store your true feelings and beliefs. To be really whole, you need to have right thoughts, the right belief system intact and walk according to the agreement about those thoughts. I call this process alignment. This is why when any two people or more agree on anything, that thing, those thoughts are done in heaven or other teachers say done in the Spirit. It will only be a matter of time for the manifestation to show up in a material way. Source, which is God, (my father God), knows all things and is ready to have his will done on earth as it is already done in heaven.

AGREE WITH WHAT IS LOVELY AND PURE

Our job is to get in alignment with the thoughts of God. Let me try to map out what the process may look like in simple terms. Alignment means to agree with good reports. Agree with what is lovely. Agree with what is Pure. Agree with positive thinking. Get in alignment with the fact that the "Lord is my shepherd or source and I will have no lack of any good thing." It is so amazing that as I write to you, a fresh awareness of God, the Source of all things is willing and ready to gives us the desires of our heart. When you set your mind, your thoughts, beliefs, and emotions into action, you create intention in the world. Once this is done, you will move, act and live according to these intentions. Oh, how beautiful and what beautiful lives we were meant to live on planet earth. Now, yes NOW, you are walking out your positive beliefs and living in accordance to what you know to be right, good and honorable. This is the greatest wisdom of all time; walking in right thinking, creating good vibrations that match God thoughts or God faith, getting on his frequency or staying positive, some teachers call it staying on the high flying discs; (Teachings of Abraham-Hicks). Being on the right "Frequency" is like getting on the right radio dial, listening to right words. There is a saying I learned about 2 years ago. It is called "Staying in the Vortex." Too me this means to stay in the presence of God or stay in a peaceful place where you can believe in your hopes and in your dreams. Next, you will need to agree with God or Source, which is the same thing as walking in alignment with God. Alignment means right thinking, right speaking and right actions brings right results. That's manifestation! The Law of attraction says you will attract what you meditate on into your life. God has made the divine process just that easy.

So, why don't most of us see Prosperity, love, joy and peace in our lives every day? Why are not more of us getting up and staying up? Why do we, who call ourselves believers not walk in this kind of Authority, power or dominion? I have found out the Secret of why most of us do not have powerful manifestations of our desires.

My journey to healing my life has been a continuous journey. I have had to learn and keep on learning. This is how I got up out of the mess I was in. And I am still learning how to get up and on top of many other situations that come my way. Your Mess is called contrast. (Teachings of Abraham/Esther Hicks). Your Mess is called problems, trouble or just plain "stuff." As long as we are in these physical bodies, we will deal with a few issues, but it is how we handle them or how we allow them to affect us that really matters most.

REMAIN IN THE VORTEX OF HIS PRESENCE

I have put my own order in to the universe and I know in my heart that I will receive my manifestation. (Pastor Rickie G. Rush-May I have my order Please). I know I am thinking and working through my path of higher thoughts and vibrations. I am fine tuning my mind to the right station or frequency through bible teachings, faith based reading and spiritual teachings and meditation. I am remaining in the God kind of faith, in the Vortex of his presence. Can't you feel all of his love, peace, joy, favor, grace, mercy and goodness? It also means maintaining an expectation of what you believe to be true, holding fast to that which is good. I know my order will be filled and that it is on its way. I am remaining full of expectation. You see, the prosperity, the nice house and the heated hot tub and beautiful spa scene, all that love, joy and peace are my dreams and I shall have what I think in my heart and what I say with my mouth. As a man thinketh, (mankind or person) keeps on thinking in his heart, so she is. Just put your order in and it shall be filled. But only if you can get there in your mind first and believe it in your heart.

I remember when I was 23 years old and heard a life changing statement. It was around 1984, my first husband, (the character "Tyrone") and myself were at a seminar when the teacher; a Caucasian male who was very centered mentally and emotionally, also financially fit made this bold statement. "You are right now, exactly where you want to be and you have right now, exactly what you want to have." I was so angry at him for telling me that my life was the sum total of my thoughts. I yelled and screamed on the inside and I did not want to go up and greet him after the meeting. I reasoned, "He doesn't even know me or my situation, how can he tell me I have what I want and I have created this mess that I am in." There I was in a room filled with people from all walks of life. At this time in my life, I was married to a man that abused me. Also, at the time, I didn't know about the law of attraction and how my poor self-esteem, poor self-image had brought him into my life. We were living as the working poor. "How could this teacher dare say such a thing about me? "Well I am taking this personal, he's just judging me because I am black and poor." I said to myself. I looked at him and had feelings of embarrassment for being poor, yet intelligent; and feelings of being inadequate, yet smart. I looked at him and wondered would I ever be good enough to have a few of the good things in life like he had. Well friend, the answer is: I feel great and yes I have a few things now. I have a much better self- image and a whole lot better self-esteem. I praise God for giving me the strength to get my thinking straight and for the wisdom to act on good thoughts. I thank God for being alive on planet earth. My first husband insisted that I read positive thinking books, spiritual books, and motivational books of all sorts. It was his rule and he ruled with an iron fist. However, reading became my blessing in disguise. I had not been a reader before I met him. Neither had I been introduced to such information as the famous work called "The course in miracles."

I knew that I needed a miracle and as I began to read on the Spiritual laws, I knew my life had to change. This change began its slow metamorphosis around 1985. It was in the midst of this chaotic mess of requiring me to read books that the Divine love of God was allowing me to see some universal truth that I had never understood before. I had come to realize that the teacher I so despised, was a gift sent to me and others in the room to give us an opportunity to open up our blinded eyes.

Yes, my first husband was the will of God in my life. Our relationship was not meant to work. But God knew he could use this battered relationship to change me into the women I needed to become. "All things work together for the Good to them who love the Lord and are called for his purpose, say Romans 8:28 KJV.

There are many problems in our homes, problems on our jobs and problems in society. There are Problems about money. As we sit and meditate, sit and pray, sit and believe, and then sit and think; the answers will come. It is really that simple, but difficult for most of us to apply. If we align ourselves up with what is divine and true and began to think on these things, our lives will change for the better. What are these things? These things are found in Phil 4:8. The bible says, "Whatsoever things are true, whatsoever things are honest, whatsoever things are just, whatsoever things are pure, whatsoever things are lovely, whatsoever things are of good report; if there be any virtue and if there be any praise, think on these things." It takes discipline to think on these things. It takes discipline to have a prayer life before God. It takes determination to change negative thinking into positive thinking and thus reaping great results in our lives. When we act upon the positive thoughts of truth, honesty, justice, purity, loveliness, good reports, virtuousness, and praise worthiness; we align ourselves with the God way of thinking;

Then we will have the God of peace with us. Can you imagine living like this, in total bliss and in total peace? Wow. What a revelation. This is how we were meant to live. This is the power of a good thought life. Choose to GET UP in your thought life.

IF YOU DON'T HAVE WISDOM, ASK GOD FOR IT!

Meditation will cause you to settle the mind and allow you to enter into stability and calmness so you can make powerful and correct decisions. Then you will be able to gain wisdom for making your decisions.

Wisdom is the key to having the ability to know what to do, knowing what to decide. You can train yourself to make wise decisions. If you do not have wisdom, just ask God for it and he has promised to give it to you liberally. (James 1: 5-KJV).

When was the last time you really prayed? When was the last time you spent 15 to 30 minutes in meditation? When was the last time you used your imagination to create vision in your life?

Now, let's talk about meditation. It is a good idea to start meditating daily. Let me share with you how you may be already doing some type of meditation and how to make meditation work for you even better. We all know about worry. Worry is a form of meditating in negative thought patterns. So all you have to do is change your negative thoughts like worry into positive thoughts. Your thoughts and beliefs create your vibrations. Your vibrations are the spiritual side of you. We create from the inside out. As you meditate and become more peaceful and settle your mind, you have a more peaceful vibration.

Do you know that if you do not want something in your future, then just stop talking about it and start meditating on what you do want. Meditating on what you do want, gets rid of things in your life that you don't want. Most of us complain and complain and complain about how terrible things are in our lives and who did us wrong and how we need more money and that we don't have enough. That just through the power of meditation daily, that situation will change and you will change most of all. By knowing what YOU DON'T WANT, YOU BEGIN TO KNOW WHAT YOU DO WANT says "Abraham Hicks Teachings". Stop meditating on things that you do not want to see in your life. Focus on what you DO WANT.

CHANGE YOUR FOCUS, CHANGE YOUR OUTCOME

How do you change your focus? I am so glad you asked! You began to focus or meditate on what you would like to have in your life. What DO YOU WANT in your life?

Begin meditation for only 5 min at a time 1 to 2 times daily, then work your way up to 10 to 20 min once or twice per day. You will soon be surprise how your life will change. In the holy Bible, Philippians 4:8 (KJV) says, "...whatsoever things are true, whatsoever things are honest, whatsoever things are just, whatsoever things are pure, whatsoever things are lovely, whatsoever things are of good report; if there be any virtue, and if there be any praise, think on these things." Now that's meditation at its best. Think about THESE THINGS! Meditate on the pure stuff, the goodness, and how you live in prosperity and how peaceful your life is and how great your health is. When you call out and think about how good and how lovely you want things to be, your spirit will line up with your new belief system. Because you now think God thoughts, you can only reproduce God things. When you are reproducing something unwanted, undesired, or in other words, fleshly carnal desires; re-evaluate what you have been meditating on.

AS A WOMAN OR PERSON THINKS IN HER HEART SO IS SHE.

A belief is something you keep telling yourself over and over again and you believe it is true, even IF IT IS NOT TRUE. Remember, if you change your thinking, you will change your life. I choose to change my life and it is getting better and better. My vibrations are lining up with the word of God that I believe to be true and the word of God I speak out of my mouth. Wow! The vibrational spiritual part of me, my spirit, is lining up with what God says about me and "My Yes is God's Yes."

Now, I can ask and it shall be given. I can seek and I shall find it and I will knock and the door will be open. As a man thinks in his heart, so is he. **(Proverbs 23:7 KJV)**

Do you know where you are going? Do you know what you want in life? Have you thought about it lately? Here is a process I would like to introduce to you.

Think About what you have been thinking about! I am asking you to "THINK!"

Reflect whether your thinking is taking you higher in vibrations or lower in Vibrations. Higher vibrations cause you to feel good, more energetic and alive. Lower vibrations cause you to feel really bad with negative or low flowing energy or vibrations.

If you are on a lower vibration, (negative thinking) you must began to change your vibration by thinking on the best thoughts you can think. It may be hard to think a very high quality thought when you have been down for a while. Just go after the best feeling thought you can think. Sometimes it is hard to believe a thought like, "I am a Millionaire," "I am a best-selling Author or my house and Cars are paid for in full." These statements may be too unbelievable at first! So start with something more believable for you, then as you began to manifest, increase your imagination, dreams and visions. At first, try saying, "I make $100, 000 instead of, I am a millionaire." Try saying, "All of my bills are paid in full each month and we have $10,000 in my savings account." This statement may be more believable.

Here are some other examples in positive thinking: Instead of thinking how terrible your job is, your spouse is or how disobedient your children are, or how sick you are, began to THINK things like:

"God blessed me to wake up this morning, I have food to eat; it may not be steak, but I have some lunch meat, some noodles and some rice." Going general in your thought life or being more general in your affirmations is a way for you to keep the" appreciation" going on the bigger issue and stops you from focusing on the individual problem. Focus your thoughts and began your day with thoughts that bring peace and satisfaction. a more generalized is thinking, "I am grateful for a roof over my head, I am thankful I have a running car, I am appreciative of our city and there is no bombing here; I am thankful that I survived that tornado, the hurricane and the flood." Amen, Amen and Amen. Going general or making general thanksgiving statements helps us get on the course to higher thinking. You will have to become a master of generalizing statements when problems hit your life, your home or your job. Other examples of general statements could be;" I thank God that I am alive. I have food to eat. We have running water. We have clothes to put on our backs and shoes to put on our feet." Amen, again to that.

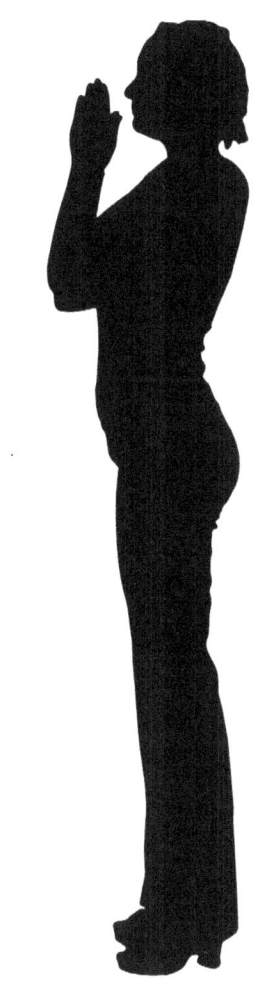

GET UP IN YOUR WORDS

Step Three *-Get Up in your Words-*

"I can't believe I said that! What? Who told you that? Girllll, did you hear the latest gossip? Well, He said that he was going to do it, but you can never believe what that person says to you." For example, the sayings go on and on. "She can never keep her word, she is always making excuses". "Child, I don't believe a word she says". "Girrrl, That's just who she is". Boy, "did you hear what they did last night?"

Dear beloved, as you read the above words, I know you may have heard a few of these statements yourself or maybe you are the one who have said them or maybe you are the one who is on the other side of the comments, the person everyone is talking about. You know, the one they are referring to who is undependable in their words. Whichever scenario you are familiar, Words are important. But how are words important? The problem we have with words are they don't always communicate truth. Most of us do not speak the truth. So we lose power in our words. We say things we do not mean. We make commitments we already know that we cannot keep or don't want to keep. The truth is, many of us play games with our words. We don't say what we mean and we seldom mean what we say in our current society. Sayings like: "Man, that's bad." Today, the word bad doesn't always mean something is "bad" or not good. Today "bad" could mean that those shoes are so "freaking beautiful." So, we have to understand words and make sure we have the proper intentions and meanings of words.

Words can heal and words can destroy. Words can build-up or words can tear down. So use your words wisely. Proverbs 31:26 says that the wise woman opens her mouth with wisdom, and on her tongue is the law of kindness. WOW! Did you know that Kindness was a spiritual law? Isn't that amazing that by using this core principle of kindness, it will yield predictable results, positive results in our lives.

THERE ARE 5 TYPES OF TONGUES I WOULD LIKE TO DISCUSS

1. The Hasty Tongue- Proverbs 29:20 says "Do you see a man hasty in his words? There is more hope for a fool than for him." Have you ever offended someone because you spoke too quickly or just had to tell your opinion and then realized you should have kept your mouth closed? Well, we all one time or another have been guilty of speaking too hastily. We all have offended people with our tongue, with our hasty words. In the bible, in the book of James 3:2, it talks about how we should control or bridle our tongue so that we will not offend others or cross verbal boundaries. "For in many things we offend all. If any man offend not in word, the same is a perfect man, and able also to bridle the whole body." I realized that in raising my two sons, both of them had different personalities and I needed to talk to them differently. Even my sisters and brothers have different temperaments. All of us have different sensitivities in certain areas of our lives and if we want to communicate effectively as women and as men, we must learn how, when and what to say to each other. Proverbs 18:13 says, "He who answers before listening-this is his folly and his shame." I must admit I had this weakness of answer-

ing before I heard the whole story earlier in my life between the ages 20 and 30. There were times on my job as a supervisor, I began to recognize that I had not heard both sides of the employee's stories before I made decisions that could affect the lives of those workers. One day I witnessed another manager doing this. He made a speedy decision and then formed an opinion about an employee before that person even told his side of the story. For the first time, I saw myself fully. I decided that I must change this defect in my speaking. Words are powerful and those said in haste can bring much unnecessary pain. We should also not make commitments in haste. We should allow a day or more if possible to make important decisions or at least give ourselves some space. If someone is pressuring you to make a decision, tell him, "Hey, I will get back with you in a couple of hours, couple of days or even tomorrow or next week." Don't be afraid to be honest and say, "I need time to think about it, I need to check my schedule at home and I will let you know by tomorrow." or whatever time YOU decide. As people of integrity, we should strive to keep our promises and commitments, so don't make them too hastily. Ecclesiastes 5:2 NKJV says "Do not be rash with your mouth, and let not your heart utter anything hastily before God."

2. The Harsh Tongue-Proverbs 15:1 "A gentle answer turns away wrath, but a harsh word stirs up anger." We can choose to go around being mean by speaking harsh words, abrasive words, sharp words or we can choose to be kind in our words. Harsh words hurt people every time. It is a form of abuse. Sometimes as parents, we can become frustrated with our kids. We can lose patience and begin to say things in the wrong voice or tone. I can remember many times when both of my sons would tell me

that I was saying some words that seemed mean to them when I got upset if they did not obey. I am sure they were describing the word "harsh." The Holy Spirit corrected me as did my children by bringing it to my attention. In fact, my two sons Sidney and Sheldon have been my greatest teachers. They taught me about myself more than anyone. They keep loving me even though I am not a perfect parent. They have loved me all the way through my transformation. I would apologize and ask for forgiveness when I realized that I had spoken to them incorrectly. Many parents do not want to apologize when they realize that they have said something hurtful to their children. Most parents know when they have hurt their children with harsh words. There is a saying that I heard while growing up, "bricks and sticks may break my bones, but names will never hurt me." This is totally a lie. Harsh words hurt and a person may find it difficult heal. Be careful with harsh words because they could be a form of verbal abuse. Whether we are talking to another adult, a relative, a friend or to our children, the same rules apply. If you have problems with speaking harshly, pray about it and ask the Spirit for help. Meditate on how you want to talk. Practice thinking about what you want to say before you start speaking. Don't speak in haste and be kind instead of harsh. Hopefully, it is not too late and you will see your loves ones respond to you in a new and positive way.

3. The Gossiping Tongue- Proverbs 18:8 says "the words of gossip are like choice morsels; they go down to a man's inmost parts. What is the definition of Gossip? In our society today, this is a big one. There are entire magazines that make their income on "GOSSIP" Nightly headlines and newspapers feature gossip columns. Now, online I've just recently seen some Christian

Gossip news that tells all the bad stuff about preachers. We are not to be the bearer of bad news or other people's business to our community. News that bring people's character down, especially when we do not know that what we "heard" is true. There are so many places where gossip can occur: On the job, at school, at the beauty shop, at the barber shop, on the phone, at the kitchen table, while cooking dinner, after church, at a party, online chat rooms; Well, Anywhere! Another point I want to make is: Do not be the trashcan for any gossiper. Stop listening to gossip about other people. Your time on the earth is limited. You are getting older and you just do not have time to waste on gossip! Do you believe that you have power in your words? Do you believe that life and death is in the power of your tongue. Why do people worry and get so interested in the affairs of other people? Why do we as people try to make other people look bad and spread rumors about other people's business? Let me ask you a question. Are you guilty of gossip? I have been guilty before, well ok, a lot of times. And I have to catch myself and go pray. I ask myself two questions. 1. Have I prayed for this person, this situation or problem that I am about to open my MOUTH ON? Well, ok, let's just all be honest, MOST of us have not prayed for the person, persons or prayed about the situation. In 2015, it is so easy to just quickly give our opinion about matters that we should first pray over to see if God is leading us to comment about them. 2. AM I really THINKING first before I talk about this person? I was just at the neurologist's office yesterday, and I did not realize that it had been two and a half years since I had been there. He said, wow, I have not seen you in a while. He said, "This can only mean that you were doing pretty good and that YOU DID NOT need my help." As I left the examination room and went into the lab office to get my bloodwork drawn, I met a wonderful lady lab tech who was an older woman and full of smiles and glowed with cheeriness. I immediately loved her energy and I told her that I was writing a book. She congratulated me and said to let her know when it came out. She shared with me that she painted artwork. I looked on her wall and she had the perfect piece of paper on THINKING that I had not seen in a while. I asked her could I use this for my book. It had no known author on it, but I was asking her to make me a copy. She did and I want to share this saying with you now so that the next time you feel the URGE to gossip, just "THINK" first. THINK stands for: T- is it True; H-is it Helpful. I-is it Inspiring; N- is it Necessary and K stands for- is it Kind. So before you gossip, is what you are about to SAY really True, Does it Help the listener, Does it Inspire the listener, is it even Necessary for you to discuss this person or situation and is it a Kind thing to say about another person and would YOU feel it was a kind thing to hear said about you? OUCH!!!

4. The Cynical Tongue-I Samuel 17:28-29 Do you remember Eliab? He was David's oldest brother. David was the one who killed the Giant, Goliath in the bible. In I Samuel 17:28-29, states, "Now Eliab his oldest brother heard when he spoke to the men; and Eliab's anger burned against David and he said, 'Why have you come down? And with whom have you left those few sheep in the wilderness? I know your insolence and the wickedness of your heart; for you have come down in order to see the battle." But David said, "What have I done now?" Cynicism is negative conversation. It is seeing the worst in a situation and complaining about a person or situation in a negative way. It can involve getting others involved with one's verbal opinions

and encouraging them to speak negatively against someone or to speak negatively about the situation. There is a saying that goes like this: "one bad apple will spoil the entire bunch." David decided to ignore his brother Eliab. I am so glad he did, because David was in the right place at the right time. He heard about an opportunity and he took that opportunity. He heard that the King of Israel wanted someone to step forward and kill the threat to the army and people of Israel. David was not afraid and he even questioned, "Why hasn't somebody gone out there and killed that Philistine Giant?" The soldiers were too afraid and so was his brother. After David heard about the generous reward that he would receive; and that he would also get a wife, David said yes to his destiny. The rest is history! If David would have kept on listening to the voice of cynicism, I wonder what would have happened.

5. The Betraying Tongue-Proverbs 11:13-says, "A gossip betrays a confidence, but a trustworthy man keeps a secret. Can you keep your best friend's secret? Can you keep your husband's or wives' secret? Or do you just have to tell it? A betrayer tells the enemy your secrets. In the United States of America, when a military soldier or officer sells secrets to another country, this is called treason! When a personal friends sells you out and gives your enemy your personal information, this is relational treason! Has anyone betrayed you? Have you betrayed anyone? There is no hurt like the hurt of someone you were very close to, someone you had shared your innermost thoughts with, someone who you thought would always be your best friend; someone who got next to your heart and whom you shared your vulnerabilities with. Then, when they go TELL YOUR STUFF-one can truly feel betrayed. Painful isn't it? Did I say that was painful? Well,

yes it is! Treason hurts! Betrayal hurts! The bible says in St John 18:2, "Judas betrayed Jesus." Judas developed a code. He would betray Jesus with a KISS. It would be the kiss that let his enemies know, "this is the man!" This crap angers me as I write. I am mad at Judas right now. I know that he is dead and buried, but he failed Jesus when he needed him the most. Betrayal can be the greatest of hurts in life. He gave in to "The Mighty Dollar." As we would say today. I know it was told in the Old Testament that somebody was going to betray Jesus. But dog gone it, did it have to be ONE of the 12 Apostles, one of the men in leadership who was very close to him? Can I give you some friendly advice right now? Friends, don't let it be you! Leaders, don't let it be you! Wives, don't let it be you! Husbands, don't let it be you! When betrayal is going down with your family or your friends, just don't let it be you! Ok, now that is out of my system! To kiss someone and know that you don't mean it, to kiss someone as a sign to someone else that I am selling this person out; to use a kiss, which is meant to be a very intimate expression to betray another is so low down. I believe this is the reason Judas later committed suicide because he realized the powerful significance of what he had done. If you have had the sting of betrayal, I am asking you to forgive the person. What? Yep, forgive! Releasing a person from the betrayal is the easiest way to move on with your life. Otherwise, you will become bitter, full of anger and risk developing rage. Turn that person over to Daddy God. The bible says, "Vengeance is mine says the Lord and I will repay." Now, if you are the person who has betrayed someone, I am asking you not to commit suicide. Our God is a merciful God full of Grace and loving kindness. He will forgive you if you repent, change your heart and start your life over. You can get up again and HAVE THE LIFE YOU DESERVE AS WELL. Here are a list of five more types of tongues and the bible scripture that goes along with it. Take time to look these up and study them and ask yourself if you need to change or need to improve in one of the areas of the tongue below.

6. The Cursing Tongue-James 3:10
7. The Complaining Tongue-Psalm 142:1-2
8. The Discouraging Tongue-Job 29:24
9. The Doubting Tongue-Mark 11:23
10. The Silent Tongue-Ecclesiastes 3: 1, 7

As you walk on this journey, ask yourself daily, "Am I walking in forgiveness today, or am I thinking, saying and acting in the vibrational harmony that will cause the manifestation I desire?" So, let me say this. Nothing changes until you decide for it to change. When we change our thoughts, then the WORDS will have to follow. For example, when we as people get tired of being broke; I mean really tired, we will do something about it. When we as people get tired of poor relationships and bad communication, then we will seek answers to our relation and communication problems. The scriptures say, "As a man thinketh in his heart so is he," (Proverbs 23:7) In other words, whatever we have been thinking on, meditating on and contemplating on will manifest through our words and in our actions. What is truly in our hearts will come out of our mouths. Our attitudes will change as our thinking and words change. Our inappropriate behaviors will be inspired to right action as we align our thinking and speaking. We can change our lives through positive, powerful and intentional words that will create the life of our dreams.

A MIND IS A TERRIBLE THING TO WASTE

During my high school years I had heard how important thoughts were. I heard the saying that went like this: "a mind is a terrible thing to waste." However, the true understanding of these words and the power to deliver ultimate freedom were not broken down to me. It was much later in my life that the understanding of these words came home to me. For example, I knew that people in our society still held themselves back with the thoughts of racism. And yes it is true that others applied the principles of racism because of their thoughts, beliefs and judgments. Society has suffered throughout history because of limited thinking and has been held in bondage due to limiting beliefs. As an African American woman and wanting to learn more about myself and my black history, I studied the effects of slavery on the black family. Limiting beliefs like prejudicial attitudes because of a person's race really hurts people and has caused poor relationships for centuries.

Do you know that the way you think gives power to your words? What have you been thinking about? You don't have to tell me. If you hang around a person for a couple of days, the REAL YOU will emerge through your WORDS. People will always show you with their mouth what they have been thinking about. Just observe and LISTEN. Soon, out of the heart, their mouth will speak.

We speak out of our hearts, especially when we are under pressure. I cannot count the times I have heard people say to someone, "I am going to give you a piece of my mind," And then their mouths uncover the thoughts of their mind. Your conversations reveal much about you, good or bad.

DO YOU REALLY KNOW WHO YOU ARE?

As I have said previously, all of us have our mindset or our belief system. Many of us do not even realize what we believe or why we SAY the things we say. It is usually when trouble comes knocking on our door, we respond from a place in our belief system; we react from how we have been trained to respond. We mostly respond unconsciously and this reveals who we really are. Do you really know who you are? **Start watching and examining your words for 30 days; you will be amazed at some of the stuff that you say.**

TAKE THE 30 DAY CHALLENGE

I was so shocked at myself when I did this little project. It's called the 30 day word challenge. Go ahead and take the challenge.

30 days of listening to yourself. Get a journal and write down your negative words, profane words and self-doubting and sabotaging words. Also note the empowering words you now use about your life and your surrounding situations. Can you choose even more powerful words? You are going to have one big eye opener if you take this 30 day challenge.

TEN SPIES BELIEVED THAT THEY WOULD BE AS TINY ANTS

There is a story in the bible that talks about 12 spies. In the book of Numbers, chapter 13 it says that 12 spies went out to spy out the land that God had given them. In the story, God had already told the 12 tribes that this land already belonged to them. All they had to do was to go into this new land called Canaan and possess it or take it like their God had instructed them.

These 10 spies came back with fear and unbelief. Out of their mouths came words of defeat and a declaration that the people who were already in the land were "Giants." The 10 spies believed that they would be as tiny ants to these giant people. Nevertheless, there were only 2 spies left to give their report. These two spies spoke boldly and declared this: "We are well able to take this land." The people became confused and began crying out and chose to think about their possible deaths and were afraid to go take the land that the almighty God had told them was already theirs.

There was only one little problem. They felt paralyzed! Fear had gripped their hearts and their minds! Their mindset had changed. Their thinking had changed through a report from 10 spies who believed that all of the people would be killed. Their thinking did not match the same vibration as God's thoughts. With this defeated thinking and pessimistic attitude, they could not go into this "Promised Land." This was the land that they had been waiting on from their God, Jehovah Jireh. Because of their mindset, they could NOT receive the land God had promised to them. Fear kept them from "a land flowing with milk and honey."

FEAR-FALSE EVIDENCE APPEARING REAL

Why were they stuck in fear- "false evidence appearing real?" Because, if they could not see it, then they could not have it. It is important to know that what you hear can affect and infect your thinking! They received a negative report. This report affected them and infected them to the point of being afraid of "Giants."

MAKE A LIST OF YOUR IMPOSSIBLITIES!

Let me ask you some questions. Who is whispering in your ear? Who is giving you a negative report-one that goes against the fiber of your being; a report that contradicts your faith, your intentions and your plans for success? You can have what you say. You can have what you see. You can have what you believe. You can have what you think. As a man thinks, so is he. What problems are you going through that seem impossible? Make a list of your impossibilities. Then begin changing your thoughts around those impossibilities. As your vibrational thoughts change, so will your words. As your words change, so will your life.

THEY DECIDED TO DO THE IMPOSSIBLE-THEY GOT UP

The words, "Why sit we here and die" came from a bible story of four men with leprosy, 2 Kings 7:3-9. They walked into a foreign city during wartime and found it empty of people, yet all of the wealth and food was still in the city. There were certain rules about people with leprosy. They could not mingle with the other people. One day something miraculous happened to them. They realized they had an opportunity to go into their enemy's camp site and take possession. They had noticed that there had not been any activity in that campsite. It was quiet and nobody had been coming in or going out. They were starving. This looked like an opportunity they could seize! But WAIT! THEY HAD LEPROSY! They were not supposed to GET UP AND TAKE OVER STUFF! They decided to DO the unthinkable; do the IMPOSSIBLE! THEY GOT UP!

They did not find any enemies left at this camp site and these four leprous men were the only ones who knew about it. Before they made the decision to see what was going on in this camp, they struggled with who they were as lepers. They struggled for their life as they sat there in a position of dying of hunger. They asked themselves, "should we continue to just sit and starve to death or should we get up and do something about our situation?" Finally, they came to the conclusion, "why sit we here and die?" In our language of today, it may have been VERBALLY SAID or THOUGHT to themselves something like this: "Why are we still sitting up here and not doing anything about our sorry situation, Nobody else is coming to help us, so we had better get up and do it for ourselves."

That one decision opened up a new reality for them. One day they were poor, but the next day they were rich. (I FEEL LIKE PREACHING RIGHT NOW!) One day they were hungry, and then the next day they had all they wanted to eat.

When we can think ourselves out of problems, tight situations and hard times, we can choose to change our outcome. Stop whining about your situations and go home and think. There are too many people who do not think. They react to situations. People don't think because it is hard work. You haven't had any hard work until you have had to think and figure out how to solve problems. We have to figure out how to get the bills paid, figure out how to send the kids to college, figure out how to take care of a dying sister, figure out how to save a troubled marriage.

YOUR WORDS MATTER

Your life now consists of how you have thought about the things in your world. If you will make better decisions, you will have a better life. As I reflect back over my own life, I see how I could have chosen better decisions. Many of my decisions were made out of ignorance, immaturity, and fear. Many of us make decisions even when we are angry, that's never good. So, like the men with leprosy, decide to make a better decision. Decide to make a better life.

Your words matter! You must realize today that what you say, decree and declare can change situations in your life. Praying can be done either with thinking thoughts or with saying words. As we speak our prayers forth, we change the atmosphere. Learn to be sensitive in your words to pray words that heal, encourage and transform you and those that listen to your words. There is another thing to note; praying will also begin to cause you to be sensitive to hearing directions from the spirit, from God.

About 10 years ago I was listening to a famous pastor on cassette tape. He was speaking on the tongue and told a story about his grandmother. He said she always went around saying "I'm going to get Alzheimer's because my mother had Alzheimer's." She constantly said this until one day she was diagnosed with that disease. This pastor stated that he realized how she created this disease. She was speaking forth what she feared. She kept saying what was on her mind and what was in her thoughts. Using your creative imagination in prayer should assist you in developing your wisdom muscles. Prayer expands your imagination and helps you to understand that there are things you can have and places you can go, even when you DO NOT SEE IT IN THE PHYSICAL WORLD. As you elevate your mind through imagination and prayer, your ability to see in the spiritual realm will increase. You will begin to gain powerful revelations from God.

WHEN WE SPEAK WORDS WE ARE CREATING OUR LIVES

In Colossians 3:2, it says that we must set our affections on things above and not on things on the earth. In other words, to set your mind on things above is a spiritual thing. It is a call for higher thinking. There is a saying in the motivational speaking world that says, "If you can change your thinking, then you can change your life." Another way of saying this is: "If you can change your mind, you can change your life." When we speak words, we are creating our lives. What we speak out comes from our thought life. The scripture says, "OUT OF THE HEART, THE MOUTH SPEAKS," (see the book of Proverb).

Matthew 4:17 is a scripture in the bible where Jesus says, repent for the kingdom of heaven is at hand." Repent means to change your mind for the better. Repent means to heartily amend your ways. I was just thinking of the many patients whom I have worked with in the mental health field. Many patients who have the diagnosis of schizophrenia say they hear voices. In fact this is one of the main determining factors of this diagnosis. The patients say cannot tell if the voices are coming from a real person or not. Many times patients have said they just want the voices to stop talking to them. Medically, it is a diagnosis that one only gets if he or she hears voices and the voices are telling them to do this or to do that; things like harming themselves or other people. These voices are the guiding instrument that lead the doctor to prescribe psychotropic medications. In other words, I am saying that we who are walking a higher spiritual path must decide not to be spiritual schizophrenics. "Listening to different voices and being unable to detect the Spirit's voice." We were created to hear the voice of God as we gain closeness to God through prayer and meditation.

We must begin to Repent. This word simply means to change your mind about something you once thought was true, but now realize it is not. Repent means to change your belief about something. To repent means to think differently about something. In this case, I want you to Believe in yourself. Know that you can achieve your dreams, hopes, and desires. Repent for having low self-esteem, repent for having low self-confidence, and repent for not loving yourself.

Start believing that you are worthy of all of God's goods." I have been encouraging lots of people these days to make dream boards or another name for it is "vision boards." I have shared this strategy with my own children, teens at the girls and boys clubs, people on my job and other people I run into. All you would have to do is began to write your vision and began to get clarity. In other words, keep it plain and simple and began to speak your dreams out loud in a spiritually charged atmosphere! Gather photo's online or cut pictures out of magazines that embody your dreams, goals or ideas of the life you want. Began to speak to yourself or out loud about your vision board you have created. Proverbs 29:18 says "Where there is no vision the people perish" (KJV).

Check out the book "Imagine Big" by Terri Savelle Foy who talks a lot about dream boards. On page 147 in her books she writes, "Stop speaking destructive words. If you think your dreams are impossible, and say that out loud, they will be impossible. If you talk about how you'll never have enough money, you never will have money. If you continually tell yourself that losing weight is so hard, it will be hard. Our words have real power. What we say will be."

Terri is an Ordained Minister and works alongside her dad, a well-known evangelist, Jerry Savelle. On page 147 of her book Imagine Big she states, "Consider how greatly we can be affected by others' words. Their words can wound our spirits deeply, or they can inspire us to do incredible things. They can fill us with deep compassion; or fill us with intense fear. Now think about how heavily influenced you are by that voice in your head. You can talk yourself into or out of just about any mood or decision. You can convince yourself that you are sick when you aren't; and with positive affirmation, you can get better when you're sick."

PRAYING POWERFUL WORDS ARE IMPORTANT

Praying powerful words are important too. You must realize today that what you say, decree and declare can change situations in your life. Praying can be done either with thinking thoughts or with saying words. As we speak our prayers forth, we change the atmosphere. Learn to be sensitive in your words to pray words that heal, encourage and transform you and those that listen to your words. There is another thing to note; praying will also begin to cause you to be sensitive to hearing directions from the spirit, from God. Prayer is a big Subject all by itself and I am not even going to try to do any justice with it in this book. However, Dr. Myles Munroe; (deceased) whom my husband Ron and I were so privileged to meet in 2012 at The Christian Center in Lawton, Oklahoma wrote a book on Prayer called Daily Power and Prayer-365 day devotional. This is only one of many books he wrote. (By the way my heart still hurts of his untimely death; he was a gift to the world).

He wrote in his introduction on page five, he says "In this devotional, I have isolated two of the most important themes of the word of God: prayer and vision. Each of these areas can vitally impact life on planet earth and must be understood, explored, and practiced for personal and corporate success."

He continued to write, "I discovered these precepts and know that prayer works and can be achieved by anyone who is willing to embrace them. I have experienced the power of vision as I have captured the dream in my heart and pursued it with all diligence. I learned priceless principles that took me from where I was to where I am today and discovered that those principles are available to every human and will guarantee the same results to all who are willing to apply them."

TERRI SAVELLE WROTE OUT A PLAN FOR HER LIFE!

I like what Terri Savelle wrote in her book "Imagine Big" on page 107. She wrote out a plan for her life, her dreams, and her vision of what she needed to change in her life. I started doing this in 2012 and my life began to change drastically. This is what she said to do in her book and it worked for me. She states, "I wrote down five things. First, I wrote down that I needed to plan for my faith, to solidify my relationship with

God. Second, I realized I needed a plan for my family, to structure my home life. Third, I needed a plan for my finances, to secure our future. Fourth, I needed a plan for my fitness, to stabilize my health. And, fifth, I needed a plan for my free time and my friends, to support my personal growth."

After reading this, I realized that her plan covered-Faith, Family, Money, Fitness and Fun! I decided that this was doable, and I needed major changes in my life.

Terri Savelle began doing this for 21 days. She said the change was slow at first, but within 21 days she started to notice new habits. Little by little over time as she worked on her plans daily, she began to change her life. Now she is a world-class motivational Christian speaker, teacher and preacher who speaks hope to millions. She measured her goals each week and each month to see that she was on track. She put up what she called a time-map so she could break down her goals into bite sizes and the date she wanted to reach them.

Another author and first lady, Dr. Bridget E. Hilliard wrote a book called My Thoughts on Victorious Confessions. She stated in her book on page 22 her personal daily confession that she prayed over her family. She writes, "I am a capable, intelligent, virtuous woman. I live the overcoming life. I live in daily expectation of abundance for my life. Every need in my life is met. I have a sound mind. I live a long life because I am redeemed from the curse of the law. I walk in divine health and healing is my covenant right. I am redeemed from the curse of the law; because I dwell in the secret place of the most high and abide under the shadow of the Almighty, No Plague come nigh my dwelling place. He redeems my life from destruction; I overcome with my faith. My mind is alert, my body is strong all the days of my life. I live a life of purpose and fulfillment; I am a blessing to the Kingdom of God. I will live to be 120 years old because God promises to satisfy me with long life and the number of my days shall be 120. I love my husband and do him good all the days of his life." What an amazing daily confession!

DR. BRIDGET HILLIARD USED CONFESSIONS DAILY

This is an awesome confession that Dr. Bridget Hilliard uses daily. It brings me such excitement when I read it that I just had to share it with you here. Her book is full of great confession over many areas of your life and it would be of value to you if you just picked up a copy. In her book she is sharing personal testimonies and how she overcame her most devastating situations. She assists her husband, Pastor Ira Hilliard with Life Change Ministries in Houston, Texas.

In 2012 I started my dream/vision board and started to do more spiritual confessions. I mixed my words with faith confessions based on the word of God. I visualized what I wanted for my life. I thought about my goals every day. I saw myself doing what I wanted to do before I actually did it. In other words; you must "see it" (Visualize it) BEFORE you can SEE IT! By 2013, I was so excited, I could see month by month that something on my list would get checked off. I saw progress! I was beginning to see my dreams, vision and goals come true. You can FORGIVE Yourself. You can FORGIVE those who hurt you. You can start THINKING powerful positive thoughts and you can begin to SPEAK powerful positive WORDS that move you into powerful positive ACTION. All of this combined will give you a Powerful Positive Life and you are well on your way to Healing your heart and getting Up Again and having the life you deserve. Now let's talk about FAITH.

GET UP IN YOUR FAITH

Step Four -*Get Up in your Faith*-

What does healing from abuse and hurt have to do with Faith? Well, the fact that you have the audacity to believe that you can be healed from a broken heart is some kind of FAITH. When I think about the word Faith, I cannot help but think of my biblical training and how I was taught about faith. My mind goes immediately to the book of Hebrews where it says in Heb 11: 1-6, "Now faith is the substance of things hoped for, the evidence of things not seen." (KJV.) Let me break this down in everyday language for you. Let's say that you are hoping to be healed from abuse. You cannot see how you will get out of that relationship, but you know that some kind of way, there is a greater power, higher power that will see you through. Personally, I called on the name of Jesus, my heavenly big brother; I called on daddy God, my heavenly Father. Whatever you do or whomever you call on has to be bigger than you. Faith is the evidence that hope is alive and well on the inside of you. Yes, you've got to have, Hope. Hope in your heart allows you to put your feet on the floor in the morning. Hope in your heart allows you to wake the kids up one more day. Hope in your heart allows you to go on that job, start that business, go back to college and even leave that man if you need to. Hope gives you a reason for Living. Hope is the evidence that you have faith coming to YOUR HOUSE. You cannot see faith, but it will manifest as the physical thing you are believing God for.

FAITH IS YOUR INGREDIENT

Faith is the substance, or ingredients that will get you the thing you are hoping for. The THING that you are hoping for in this example is...Let's say a cake. The cake (the thing that you want for your birthday party...) has flour, salt, baking powder, sugar. Let's call these elements the DRY ingredients. Dry ingredients are necessary for your faith walk. The dry parts make up your Faith foundation. The cake, which is the thing you are hoping to get in this birthday party example, needs also the wet ingredients: eggs, milk flavor, butter...oh yea, lots of butter! When all of these substances come together, we have us a cake batter. That cake batter is the faith substance. We are hoping that it will make us a cake, yes we are wanting to eat us some cake. We are praying that it will taste good and that we have mixed it all up just right. How is your faith right now? Is it weak? Is it shaky? Is it about to give up? Wait, don't throw it away. I write on these pages to tell you to HOLD ON!

IT IS NOT OVER YET! LETS GET SOME FAITH IN YOUR

Why is it not over yet? Because there is still another PROCESS that the cake batter must go through in order for it to become a real nice, beautiful cake that YOU can eat. That process is called the OVEN process. The cake batter has to be BAKED. See ladies, so many of us claim to have faith, but we do not want to GO THROUGH ANY PROCESSES, ESPECIALLY THE BAKING PROCESS. The fire in the oven has got to be set on a temperature that will make sure the cake will rise to the occasion. I set most of my oven temperatures to 325- 350 depending on the recipe. Sometimes if I am making a small single cake, I set the temperature higher. But if I am making a double recipe, I will have to use a bigger baking dish and I set the temperature to 325, a little lower temperature. While it is baking, I make sure that the cake is cooked all the way through. That way, we can say that it is done. There is nothing like a great cake that has the right moisture when you taste it, along with the right amount of flavor and sweetness. YOU MUST HAVE THE FAITH TO BAKE YOUR CAKE which will represent the things or the dreams in your life or we could just say "YOUR LIFE."

When you "bake your life," many people will be able to take a slice of it and they will say how delicious your life is to them. You will be a living testimony of healing from hurt, pain and shame. You will walk as a living manifested miracle for others to see.

Have you heard about the story in the bible of a man named Lazarus? Jesus loved his friends: Lazarus and his two sisters. They took care of Jesus every time he came through their part of the country. You know there is nothing like good friends. I am talking about the ones who have your back. Yes, the friends that act the same every time they see you. REAL sistah girlfriends. Not the two-faced type who are jealous of your success. Happy when you were down, but now that you got up again, they are mad with their noses stuck in the air and are talking about you. Well, Jesus had him some REAL friends. They had his back and he had theirs! But one day Lazarus died. They sent for Jesus, but it seemed like he took his time coming! He stopped along the way to heal some other people he did not even have a close relationship with. He did not make it in time to pray a healing prayer over Lazarus. These two sisters felt disappointed and sad that their brother had died. Where in the heck was Jesus, Mary and Martha WONDERED? If Jesus would have just hurried up and laid his anointed hands on Lazarus, he would have been healed. They believed that prayer could change things!

THE TWO SISTERS THOUGHT IT WAS TOO LATE!

Well, by the time Jesus got there, their brother was dead and buried. The two sisters were really upset with Jesus and said it was TOO LATE! But Jesus told them to: "take me to his grave, take me to where you laid him, and take me to where you covered him up. They told Jesus, "it is too late, he is stinking by now." "Why do you want to go their Jesus? WHY?"

But Jesus went there ANYWAY! Jesus called him by his name. He had FAITH to raise Lazarus up from the dead. Lazarus got up. LAZARUS WAS RESURRECTED FROM THE DEAD! He was wrapped up in his grave clothes, but as he began to walk, the grave clothes came off of him. Layer by Layer, the grave clothes came off and he was set free. As he gained strength, he walked up and down the street and throughout his area being an example for his peers to see that God sent THE WORD. The Word was walking and talking and the Word's name was called Jesus. He came into that city just because of Lazarus. Jesus came to speak a word over that deadly and mournful situation. The Word was FULL of faith, enough to raise a man named Lazarus from the dead. Lazarus, GET UP! Rise up! LIVE!

Well, I am talking to you right now, Male or female. If you feel like your life is over, if you feel like your life is dead. If you feel like you could never really live fully again. I just want to speak a quiet piercing word into your ear and say: GET UP, YOU CAN BE HEALED, GET UP, YOU ARE SET FREE. Go ahead and set your mind free. Forgive, change your negative thoughts to positive thoughts; change your negative words to positive words; change your unforgiveness to forgiveness and let FAITH step in and heal you. Let your heart be healed. Allow God and Faith in God to resurrect your life. You can be healed from your emotional pain and you can get up and live fully again. Have faith!

Now, Go ahead and take the blender and thoroughly mix up you some faith. Let the process of Faith bake you- Yes bake you inside of Heaven's oven. Let the Universal God move his finger of faith over you and make you "well done," ready to be sliced and served to mankind.

I THINK ABOUT THE BIBLE'S HALL OF FAME!

I also think about the bible's hall of Fame, where it names all of the men and women who got their name on the roll! Wow, how awesome to be a woman and get your name in the Bible's hall of fame. Women in the bible days did not have all of the fantastic rights that we as women have today. Just to see a woman listed in the bible as a woman of significance makes me proud. So, whether in the faith hall of fame or just mentioned for their roles in the scriptures, women were important in the development of faith.

I love to talk about Mary, the mother of Jesus. She was the only mother in history that got to feel her baby twice. When the Holy Spirit put the baby Jesus in her womb, this was a miracle-an amazement. She was chosen out of millions to carry the anointed one-The Christ. She was the only mother that got to carry the same baby twice. Through faith and the filling of the Holy Spirit on the day of Pentecost, Jesus's mother, Mary received the awaited promise, the Holy Spirit. By faith she waited in the upper room. She waited! She was God's earthly mother. She had gone through so much. God had trusted her and Joseph to take care of the "Holy One." He trusted her to walk by faith. She had to be infused with faith to say yes to an assignment that was too hard to handle by herself. Mary, the mother of Jesus said "yes" to this assignment- which would include rejection, months of rumors, looks of despisement, doubts about of her virginity and questions about her character.

She carried the baby Jesus to full term despite the questions of doubt and rejection even by her husband to be of her "faithfulness to him." It was only after an angel came to him as the story goes, and gave him insight that he too received faith to believe that Mary was carrying the "anointed one."

He stayed with her throughout the birth of Jesus and supported her and the baby Jesus. They had to leave the area where they lived because of threats on baby Jesus's life. They went through some hard times, even though they were called to walk by faith. How do we know they went through some hard times? She had to have her baby in the back of a barn. The hotels were all full and nobody felt sorry for this young couple. How cruel it would seem that nobody would give up their room for a woman who was pregnant about to give birth. Cruel and hard as it was, they stood the test of Faith. She delivered her baby and God supplied their needs. They were not blessed with a nice hotel room that night. Wow, is all I can say. Sometimes, what we pray for or hope for does not always look like what we have been praying for. But keep walking by Faith. People, family or friends may criticize what God has told you to do! But keep on walking, even if you have to sleep out in the back; inside of a barn. When you know that you are doing all that you can do and that you have turned it over to God, he will not fail you. Your faith will not fail you. Just start gathering all of your ingredients for baking you that cake. By faith you can go further than you can even dream you can go.

Many times we as women have to be willing to get up and move to another area of town or even go to a new city. In the above case of Mary and Joseph; her husband helped her start life over. She had faith to get up without a job promise, without a career offer and do whatever it was to walk in her destiny. She did what she had to do to get the job done.

Her job in this situation was to protect the baby Jesus and to keep him safe from people who were trying to kill him. She was walking by faith. She was clear about her beliefs. She was clear about her intentions. She knew what her assignment was in life and she was willing to pay the price for her family to be successful.

Who's trying to hurt you? Who is hindering you? Who is threatening you? It may be time to MOVE on, MOVE over or MOVE OUT! You can get up with faith on your side.

HERE ARE A FEW ACTION STEPS OF FAITH:

1. Get clear about what it is you really want to do
2. Pray about what you want to do. Then ask God/ or your higher power for wisdom (The bible says that in all your getting, get understanding.) Proverbs.
3. Consult wise counsel- Either from a group of trusted friends who are wise and know you and who have your best interest at heart. Also seek professional help if you need a professional point of view on the matter or if you don't have wise trusted friends or family.
4. Make a plan to leave. However, you are in a dangerous situation, you must be careful. Get out of harm's way immediately of course if your life is on the line or if a lover, husband or boyfriend has threatened you or has threatened your family.
5. Start seeking another living situation if it has come to that. Start looking early and save up some money if your life has become uncertain and abuse is present. Sometimes it is better to live below your means for a while. This may mean living with a friend, a family or in a group home situation. Your safety is all that matters. Your healing is what is important. Your sanity is on the line. Nothing is worth your sanity. Leave things behind if necessary. You can get back things such as furniture, cars and houses; but you cannot get back your life if it is taken.
6. Get help to move-family or friends are usually willing to help

you when you come clean with what is really going on in your life. You don't have to tell them everything, but as you let them know that You need to make a change for your good and that you cannot do it alone, people will began to show up for you.
7. Practice "NO CONTACT" This means not talking to the person who has hurt you. Especially when you are moving out. Your abuser may try to call you or contact you on your cell, with text message, on Facebook and other social media sites. Just take this time to relax and seek peace of mind. Rest!

I was in an abusive first marriage, and I decided to leave. Suddenly he decided he was moving too because he did not want to pay rent there anymore. I thought I had a deposit coming back from the rental property, but he beat me to it. I had put the deposit down on our rental place, but he had gone ahead of me and got the money for himself from the landlord. He never said a word to me about it. I contacted him to see if he would give me half of it, but he would not respond to me. Then one day he told me that he had gone to get the money because he needed it more than I did. I was angry about it for a while but then I began to remember that I served a God who was bigger than my problems. I had to reach out for faith, so I grabbed on to it. Money was very tight! I stayed with three different families while I was trying to get myself together. In a sense, I was homeless! I could have easily gone back home to my parent's house in Texas, but I had too much pride. I did not want my family to see me as a failure. I stayed with three different girlfriends.

I LISTENED TO PEOPLE INSTEAD OF LISTENING TO MY HEART

At first, I found a single girlfriend who had no live in boyfriends or husband. But after moving in with her, I discovered that she did have a few men or "lovers who came by to see her." Well, this did not work out because she was not getting to see her lovers like she wanted. It was clear, my presence was an interference. I had come between her and her lifestyle. She let me know that it was time for me to leave. I had only been there for about a month. I did become angry about it, but I could see that our friendship was over. She put pressure on me to leave in two weeks. I decided to leave the next day with nowhere to go. I did not want to be there anymore. The atmosphere had changed from friendly to hostile.

In the same apartment building, there was a young lady whom I had befriended while living at those apartments. I was upset and I packed my things. I went downstairs to that lady's apartment. I had occasionally seen and talked with her a few times while coming and going. We had shared small talk and I had been kind to her children. I knocked on her door just for comfort and to burn off steam about what just happened! She immediately insisted that I stay with them until I could find a roof over my head.

Her husband was in the army and they had three kids. (I had no kids at the time). Everything was constantly busy at their home. She had small kids who ran around and played, screamed and hollered like children usually do. I was too stressed to help her with the children. I could tell she was overly stressed as well with all of her responsibilities since her husband had to leave often for military duties.

There were toys everywhere. There were dishes that needed to be washed! There was laundry to be done and several meals to be cooked! All this was just normal parenting stuff for any young family raising small children, but my nerves were already wasted! I needed to find somewhere else to lay my head.

I needed peace and quietness to think. I wanted to think about my future. A long busy and noisy week had past when I met another military young woman who happened to be visiting the home of the second girlfriend. We quickly became friends in a few days. She saw my frustrations and asked me to come to live with her and her boyfriend. I moved in with them. Their apartment was quiet and I began to think about my life!

I NEEDED SOMETHING AND IT WAS CALLED FAITH

This third girlfriend had a boyfriend who was in the military. Fortunately, he was gone in the field for ten days when she asked me to move in with them. Before he returned from field duty, I had secured new employment in another city, Topeka Kansas.

I had to make a change. I needed something right then and there! IT WAS CALLED FAITH!

I had to walk by faith in a new city. I knew no one! I was scared! But I had to make me a "cake." I started to pull in all of the ingredients- job applications, searching for a new apartment, securing a down payment.

Well, I baked the cake and added as much flavor, sugar and butter as I THOUGHT should go into the batter. It was NOT a perfect sweet cake. My faith was shaky, but I did my best. Sometimes your best is all you can do. I leaned on my daddy God.

As I ventured out on FAITH and found a new job in a new city, I knew I was not healed yet, but I did not know whom to turn to for real solid counsel or advice. I was still hurt and depressed over losing my marriage and embarrassed about my ex-husband's physical and verbal abuse of me. I was still lonely. I did not want to go back to Texas as a failure. (At least in my own mind. Nobody said these words; they were my own self negative chatter).

HE TOLD ME HE LOVED ME AND TREATED ME LIKE ROYALTY

My ex-husband called. I listened! I was too nice! I chose to believe him! I was still lonely. I was UNKNOWINGLY a Co-dependent. I re-married him within a few months! He told me he loved me. He treated me like royalty. But after the FIRST MONTH of re-marriage was over, the insanity started up again! He abused Me AGAIN. My heart was crushed AGAIN!

Well, Ok, Now I see it. But back then- I was blind and thought I was in love and "doing what the church and everybody else wanted me to do." The church people said… "You know you need to try and get back together with your husband, the bible says you can't get divorce unless there was adultery."

The church people said, "Since yall didn't commit adultery, both of you can ever get married again and you can never have sex again." I wondered how they knew all of our personal intimate details in the bedroom, but I knew people loved to speculate.

YOU CAN ONLY TEACH WHAT YOU KNOW

I listened to the people instead of listening to my heart. I totally believe in the bible, but many people mis-interpret what some scriptures say. Most church people mean well. One thing I have learned is this- You can only teach what you know.

So I accepted the LIE that we were supposed to get "remarried." I entered AGAIN-back into an abusive situation where there were NO boundaries, NO counseling arranged, and I had No one to talk with about my SECRET pain.

I COULD NOT FACE THAT I WAS SUFFERING FROM LOW SELF ESTEEM

This was the law of attraction working in my life in a perfect way. I did not even know what spiritual laws like the law of attraction were all about. I DID NOT KNOW that I was married to someone who was a narcissist or who may have had a narcissistic personality disorder. I was in the dark about narcissistic and co-dependent relational abuse at my young age of 28. I DID NOT KNOW that these two types were most likely ALWAYS attracted to each other unless major growth occurred in one of the individuals.

I could not face that I was suffering from low self-esteem, low self-confidence, co-dependency issues, and poor boundary issues. I did not have a name for how I felt on the inside. I knew I wanted to love someone deeply. I wanted to believe in another person and have someone to believe in ME. I wanted someone whom I could become deeply intimate with, (not just sexual with). For the life of me, I could not make it happen.

It was faith that gave me the courage to GET UP and LEAVE HIM AGAIN!

I WAS ONLY FIVE STEPS AWAY FROM CHANGING MY LIFE

I started seeking forgiveness of myself for making a bad decision; forgiving him for being just who he was-he could not change his behaviors. He said he did not need to change!

But, I started to change my thinking. I started to change my confession-the words I said about myself and about my situation. I decided to get up again and renewed my mind to the word of God, the bible. I read as many positive thinking books I could read. I prayed, went to church and worked.

This was a new start again for me. I was finally alone-to heal; To GET UP AGAIN.

I knew deep inside myself that all of those years OF ABUSE, SUFFERING AND SHAME would not go to waste. God does not waste one drop. I did not know it then. But, I was only "five steps" away from changing my life.

It is only by the power of God that I can even write this story to you without crying and without feeling sorry for myself. I now write without guilt or shame. It is God that helped me to have the FAITH to get up again. I now live by Faith and I have a new life, fresh beginning; a resurrected life in Christ. I have Faith to live by his word. Let faith begin the healing process in you right now.

I now have the courage to say to the world that I am in recovery from domestic abuse, hurt, suffering and co-dependency. I am being continually renewed day by day. I am far from perfect, but I walk in His perfection.

God through faith will help you to get up and heal your life and have the life you deserve. Stand still and see what God will do in you and through you.

GET UP IN YOUR LOVE

Step Five -*Get Up In Your Love*-

"What's love got to do, got to do with it" says singer, Tina Turner. Now, that's a woman who has been there and done that! Her love song says, "Who needs a heart when a heart can be broken". I use to sing that part of the song every once in a while. Most of my other songs were gospel. I didn't know any other words to Tina Turner's song. But those few words would not leave my soul. I continued singing this part of the verse in my house while my kids were growing up. Every once in a while, those words would come to me and I would just start singing it out of the blue. Now, you must realize that I was raised singing gospel music all day and every day. So, it was a little strange for me to just pop out of my mouth with a Tina Turner song.

LOVE HAS NOTHING TO DO WITH YOU BEING ABUSED

I finally realized after years and years of singing this on and off, this song was asking me a personal question. The question that I knew had never been answered by me, nor had it been answered by many other women who had suffered from abuse. What DOES love got to do with IT? The answer is: Absolutely NOTHING! Love has nothing to do with you being ABUSED. But I must disagree with the part of the song that says, "Who needs a heart when a heart can be broken?" We cannot throw away our hearts, we cannot hide our hearts, and we cannot pretend that our hearts do not hurt. There is only one thing that I want to encourage you to do with your broken heart…. HEAL YOUR HEART and get back up again!

Are you in love or are you just co-dependent? Before I talk about what love is, I want to discuss with you the definition of co-dependency. Co-dependency would be when you try to get your love needs, self-esteem needs and self-image needs met through another person and you feel inadequate to meet your own needs of self-love. When another person or anybody treats you badly and disregards your needs and disrespects how you feel and you still feel the need to protect them, cover up for them and excuse their bad behavior continually, then you are co-dependent.

Co-dependency is a form of over attachment in a relationship, whether it is towards your lover, your children, your friends, or even parents; it stems from a lack of self-love and lack of self-worth. As a woman, you cannot make a man love you or do right by you. He has to have that commitment in his own heart already. He has to have this type of character and enough love to give to you as a woman he respects. He must be willing to learn to truly love you unconditionally. A quality man, a good man, a real man will not just love your body and the sex you give him. He must love all of you, both inside and out and be willing to accept you as you are.

No matter how much you love that man in your life, if he does not accept you and refuse to care for you tenderly, share his life with you, be honest, show you respect and invest in the relationship and commit to not abusing you in ALL FORMS, (sexually, emotionally, physically, financially, mentally), then he is not worth YOUR TIME OR YOUR LIFE!

Here are 9 SIGNS OF CO-DEPENDENCY

(If you have more than several, you may be co-dependent- I will let you be the judge.)

1. Sacrifice yourself by over giving. You try to make everything perfect for the takers in your life.
2. You always put other people first. You feel as if you should make things better and overlook your own needs. This may stem from a sense of "Nobody paid attention to you unless you were being helpful".
3. You have been called the mature child. You feel everyone look up to you and depend on you to step in and save the day, so you always feel the need to do this.
4. You have a hard time saying no. Growing up, you felt saying no meant that you would not be loved. You want to feel love and feel compelled to say yes, even if it is not in your best interest. Saying YES, gets you into situations you later regret.
5. Nothing you do is ever good enough. You try to please your lover, husband or wife. You feel that you try to please those on your job and your friends, but you still feel like you are a disappointment to them.
6. Crying or being sad was not accepted and it was looked down upon. You felt that you had to hold your emotions inside.
7. You cannot depend on people because they are not reliable for you. Your parents love was on and off depending on how good you were or if you met their expectations.

8. **Nobody seemed to really care about your feelings. You felt invisible or like a ghost except when they needed you.**
9. **Feeling love for you has always had conditions attached. It meant that you had to do what someone else said to get there approval. You feel your family dictated your decisions growing up.**

The bible says to love your neighbor "AS" we love ourselves. This is the key; to learn to love OURSELVES FIRST. Just like we love ourselves, we can love other people. But if we do not love ourselves, then we cannot give TRUE LOVE to other people. Now this is heavy. We must ask ourselves have we truly loved others or have we only given counterfeit love? I believe that most people do not really understand love or know what true and real love is. We use the word love in our society very loosely. We love to eat, we love to drink, and we love this church. I love your shoes, I love your house, and I love that car. This is why I want to talk about Self Love. I just don't think we know what love is. There is a song that says, "I wanna know what love is…."

My favorite love chapter in the bible is I Cor 13: 1-8. It says: "Though I speak with the tongues of men and of angels, and have not charity, I am become as sounding brass, or a tinkling cymbal. And though I have the gift prophecy, and understand all mysteries, and all knowledge; and though I have all faith, so that I could remove mountains, and have not charity, it profiteth me nothing. And though I bestow all my goods to feed the poor, and though I give my body to be burned, and have not charity, it profiteth me nothing. Charity suffereth long, and is kind; charity envieth not; charity vaunteth not itself, is not puffed up, Doth not behave itself unseemly, seeketh not her own, is not easily provoked, thinketh no evil; Rejoiceth not in iniquity, but rejoiceth in the truth;

Beareth all things, believeth all things, hopeth all things, endureth all things. Charity never faileth…" (KJV)

Charity means LOVE. My favorite part of this scripture is love suffers a long time, love is kind, love does not envy, love does not have pride, love is not puffed up, love doesn't act unprofessional or act out of character, love doesn't seek to have its own way, love doesn't get angry easily, love does not go around thinking evil of others, love does not rejoice about sin, but rejoice over the truth. Love is able to bear all things and it believes all things are possible. Love is hopeful and love has endurance. Love never fails.

This scripture is one of the most powerful verses in the bible, oh yea...did I say that already? Well, yes it is.

This word love was interpreted from the Greek language in the New Testament. There are three meanings in the bible for Love. There is the "Eros love." This is sexual love. If a person said I EROS you, then they are saying that I feel sexual love for you.

Then there is "Philia love" in the bible- this meaning has a friendship love behind it. It means I love you as a friend. Then the third meaning of Love is "Agape love." It is the ultimate kind of love from God. It is how God feels, believes and thinks about us.

The bible reads in the book of John 3: 16, "For God so "Agaped" the world that he gave himself for it." This love or the agape love is the Purest of all loves. There are no hidden agendas, nothing that you are trying to get from another person- such as sex or friendship. But it is a love that gives and sacrifices with pure intentions. This love desires the best for you and desires the highest good for mankind. As human beings, we must ask the Spirit of God to empower us to love this way. We can only do it through the power of God.

A RELATIONSHIP GONE BAD

In the Old Testament book of the bible there is a love story of a man named Samson and a woman named Delilah. (Judges 13-16) People in those days usually only preferred to marry in their own tribe. During this time in history many wars were going on between countries and different cultures of people. Dating or falling in love with someone in another culture was highly discouraged and could even mean death or at least one could be labeled a traitor or an outcast.

Samson was in one of the twelve tribes of Israel and was considered God's chosen people. Delilah was a Philistine woman and her nation wanted to destroy God's people and to bring them into captivity.

However Samson just desired and lusted after the Philistine women. His parents had warned him to stay away from these women, but Samson would not heed their advice. He loved to play with fire. And what did momma say to us about playing with fire. Yes, momma said, "if you play with fire you will get burned."

But Samson loved Delilah. She was his addiction. Like a drug, he had to have a dose of her love daily… "Eros love" of course. He could not get enough of her! Delilah loved to play games. She enjoyed deception. She was a sort of gambler. She loved money and would do whatever she could to enjoy the fruits of money, legally or illegally. Delilah was a business woman. She was not in love with Samson which made it easy when the leaders of the Philistine government asked her to find out where the strength of Samson came from. The Philistine men had tried several times to defeat this man, but no matter what they tried to do, he defeated them. They observed Samson and detected that he had a weakness and this weakness was WOMEN.

THIS MATERIAL GIRL WENT TO WORK!

So they went to this business woman named Delilah who was already using Samson. They made her a financial offer. I read in research that this offer would have made this woman a millionaire.

Now, what deceptive woman could turn down a million dollars? She accepted the offer and went to work to break Samson down. The bible says that it is "better for a man to live on the housetop than to live in the house with a nagging woman."

If Delilah lived in the twenty first century, maybe she would have been called a "Material Girl or a Gold Digger". Not just because she wanted or desired money, but because of her ethical values and her deceitfulness to obtain the money.

This "Material Girl went to work." Day in and day out she worked on Samson to give her answer to where his strength was located. She played with his emotions, lied to him, and deceived him.

The bad thing about this game was that he knew she was playing with him and with his emotions, because when the military Philistine men came in to capture him several times, they could not overtake him. Samson laughed about it instead of taking it serious!

He kept up his sexual relationship with her. Every time the men came into the house to overtake him, Samson would overpower them. She cried and said, "Samson you lied to me, please tell me your secret," she demanded. "I thought you told me the truth," she yelled out.

Samson also liked to play games. Samson, also liked to deceive. He assumed that he could "out think" his lover. He assumed that he would not allow himself to be tricked or seduced by her charm. He thought he was THE MAN AND THAT HE WAS IN CHARGE OF THE SITUATION.

But he was in love with her and that made the difference. He had given her his heart. He became blind spiritually and emotionally. He refused to see Delilah for what and who she really was.

LOVE CAN MAKE YOU DO SOME STUFF!

Love can make you say some stuff and do some stuff during intimacy that you would never say otherwise. Intimacy opens up your heart and leaves you vulnerable. This is the reason we must be careful who we are intimate with.

True sexual intimacy should be reserved for the person you have chosen for your marital mate. That mate should be trustworthy and accountable for his actions, for what you tell him or her during your time of intimacy, and for what he or she does with that information that came out of your intimate time. Sexual intimacy can open you up like nothing else can.

A true intimate partner will not take the secrets that you tell him in the bedroom-during that special time then turn around and tell your secrets to the world. This is even respected in the court of law in the United States. Wives or husbands do not have to testify against their own spouses. They are exempt. Wow!

If Samson was in the twenty first century he may have been labeled as a sex addict. A sex addict puts his needs for sex above anything else. It is "the fix" for him or her to feel good, to feel cared for or to feel needed.

A sex addict cannot stop themselves from having sex. They must have sex even it means their lives are in jeopardy. Their need for sex is more important than reputation, honor, or money at the time they need it.

This type of sex can be classified as one form of lust. James 4:1-4 "From whence comes wars and fighting's among you? Come they not hence, even of your lust that war in your members? Ye lust, and have not: ye kill, and desire to have, and cannot obtain: ye fight and war, yet ye have not, because ye ask not. Ye ask, and received not, because ye ask amiss, that ye may consume it upon your lusts. Ye adulterers and adulteresses, know ye not that the friendship of the world is enmity with God? Whoever therefore will be a friend of the world is the enemy of God. KJV

HE LOVED HER, BUT SHE DID NOT LOVE HIM!

Well, Samson's love went bad. He loved her, but she did not love him. He was wrong about her! She DID NOT change. She DID deceive him! He STAYED with her and she DID him wrong.

HE LOST HIS FREEDOM MESSING AROUND WITH THAT WOMAN

He lost his strength messing around with that woman! He lost his eyesight messing around with that woman! He lost his freedom messing around with that woman! He lost his position in his country messing around with that woman! He lost his power and authority messing around with that woman! He ALMOST lost his Destiny and Purpose for his life messing around with that woman!

It took the pain of "Love Gone Bad" for him to come to himself! He realized that it was the will of God for Him to defeat the Philistines. His destiny was delayed but not denied. He had to get back into position. He had to forgive himself and seek God's forgiveness. He finally prayed and asked God to give him strength one more time to defeat his enemies, the Philistines! God gave him the strength and he did go down in history for destroying the enemies of God.

Solomon was the son of King David. He was another man who loved strange women. He was known as the wisest man alive, but he eventually allowed his need and lust for many women ruin his judgement and spiritual values. I Kings 11: 1-3 says "But King Solomon loved many strange women, together with the daughter of Pharaoh, women of the Moabites, Ammonites, Edomite's, Zidonians, and Hittites; Of the nations concerning which the Lord said unto the children of Israel, Ye shall not go into them, neither shall they come in unto you; for surely they will turn away your heart after their gods.

Solomon clave unto these in love. And he had 700 wives, princesses, and 300 concubines: and his wives turned away his heart. For it came to pass, when Solomon was old, that his wives turned away his heart after other gods, and his heart was not perfect with the Lord his God, as was the heart of David his father. (KJV)

Solomon's lust for many women, 700 hundred who were his wives turned him away from his spiritual beliefs. He was no longer committed to the Lord God and he began to allow his wives to worship other gods and they influenced him to worship other gods as well. Simply put, when you hang around bad company you will eventually be influenced to partake of their activities.

Even though he was the wisest man on earth, his wisdom went out of the window so to speak when it came to his wives and their influence over him.

Let's face up to it women, we have influence, we have power and we can change things in our homes. Many times we as women do not realize the influence we have over our men. These women convinced a King who once served the most high living God to turn and serve statues and idols.

Now that's some power.

DISCOVERING SELF LOVE

Robert Schuller wrote in his book called "Self Love" and he states "that the real key to self-love lies in self-discovery, self-development, self-discipline and self-dedication." He states "there are ten concrete steps that will help you to become the person you want to be" In his book on page 102-113 there are steps 1- 10 as follows:

1. Get rid of your fear of failure-he states, "We are afraid to face up and honestly meet ourselves for fear we might discover we are failures, and we are afraid of failure!" "Why are we afraid of failure? We fearfully believe that our friends will forsake us if we fail." "However, you will not love yourself if you are dominated by a fear of failure. Rather, you will tend to become jealous, or hypocritical, or perfectionistic, or selfish, or aggressive, or resentful. If you turn into that kind of a negative emotional person, you will surely hate yourself."

2. Discover that unique person called you- he states, "You discover yourself in adventure, in freedom to stand on your own feet; in belonging to a family or group; in fellowship, deeply sharing your fears and hopes with people you can trust; involvement in cause you believe in deeply; in creativity, whether it is a book, a song, or a painting; in responsibility, shun responsibility and you will never discover your capabilities; in self-discipline-here you discover your hidden power."

3. Compliment yourself-he states, "As you compliment yourself you will begin the slow process of de hypnotization. For many years you have hypnotized yourself into believing the worst. Now you can break this negative spell that has gripped you for years. You start hypnotizing yourself when you start to compliment yourself. It's not easy. You'll feel boastful, vain and hypocritical-but you've got to do it." "From childhood on you have been covering your real self under layers of self-criticism. You can pull off those layers of self-condemnation and expose a great heart deep down inside!"

4. Forgive yourself- he states, "While the old paint may be stripped off, there still remain the stains of self-condemnation, regret and remorse which must be eliminated... God has forgiven you, forgive yourself."

5. Improve yourself-he states, "When you compliment yourself, you are beginning to improve your self-image by offsetting the negative qualities you may have. "You cannot always control what happens in life, but you can control your reaction to the event. Look upon every experience, whether good or bad, whether a triumph or a tragedy, as a challenge to make you a better person."

6. Accept yourself- "You've complimented yourself. You've forgiven yourself. You're learning to improve. Now get ready to accept yourself." "Accept yourself. God made you the way you are because He wanted you to be distinctive. He likes what He created. You should too."

7. Commit yourself to a great Cause- "By a commitment to people, projects or causes, you will have an opportunity to assume responsibilities. Responsibility generates self-love, for responsibility fulfills the need to be needed."

8. Believe in success- "First you need a dream, and then you will need a scheme-develop a schematic blueprint. A team is the next. No man is big enough to make a big dream come true if he's working alone. You can accomplish the impossible if you recruit the intelligence to advise you and work with and for you. Now build a beam under your dream. Support your dream with faith, hope and prayer. Now put a gleam on your dream. Dedicate your success to the service of God and to your fellowmen."

9. Strive for excellence- "Do the best, whatever you do." You'll love yourself when you know your achievement is of high caliber."

10. Build self-love in others- "This is the last step in building a strong self-love. Forget yourself now and start thinking about the people around you who think too poorly of themselves. You can give their dis-

couraged, depressed spirits a lift, and in so doing find even more reason to regard yourself as a person of worth."

These ten steps came from Dr. Robert Schuller. He is a master at teaching about self-love. Self-love is learning to appreciate yourself, having self-worth and also having self-respect. I am remembering a song growing up back when I was a teenager called, "Respect Yourself." This means you have personal dignity and you have a sense of personal self-value.

I remember learning more about personal value one day when I attended a conference put on my Bishop TD Jakes. Pastor Paula White was preaching this particular sermon when she began to talk about a vase and how we perceived its value if we just thought it was a plain vase from a department store and she talked about it being at a price that the vase could be easily replaced. Then she suddenly added that this WAS NOT a regular low cost vase but that it was now worth thousands of dollars. She said the vase was kept in the Bishop's house in a special case to be admired and that it was priceless. Then she did the unthinkable. She threw the vase to one of the ushers and said "catch."

I DECLARE RIGHT NOW, RESPECT YOURSELF

Everyone in the audience gasped! Thankfully he caught it as all of us held our breaths. OH My God! I said to myself, "I can't believe she did that." Then she said, "Now you all perceived that the vase was so very valuable and worth a lot" but when you thought that it was just from Walmart or Target you didn't feel the value of the vase. The vase was mundane and irrelevant. Her demonstration was so true, so powerful and very real as she told us later that it was NOT valued at thousands of dollars. What she wanted us to see is that we placed "value" on something when someone else has elevated the item or if we perceived the item to be "valuable." She showed us that we "felt differently" about the item and we had "reacted differently" about the item when we THOUGHT THAT IT WAS CHEAP! Yes, I declare right now, RESPECT YOURSELF, I am worthy of all of God's good. I am a virtuous woman far above rubies. Yes, women speak it loud and clear. Love yourself!

I recently met a businesswoman who is also a counselor from California and has her own private counseling service. Her name is Wendy Whitemoor. She started this program called: "I love me some ME." when I read about the program on social media, I secretly wondered, "Now, who has ever heard of a name like that, and what does she mean about loving me some me." She had informed her friends on Facebook and other social media outlets that she was having a conference tour on the subject and also 3 days of conference calls to talk about "loving me some me." I almost didn't make the call because I was almost offended at such a big bold title! I just could not quite get over that she wanted to talk about the subject of "loving me some me." The first thing that came into my mind was: "How selfish is that." I still struggled over the thought of 'ME" being the center of attention. For a co-dependent, that is a hard pill to swallow.

Co-dependents are used to catering to the needs of other people. I struggled with her title until I made the phone call on the second night and listened to the conference call. Then I called back the last night. Let me tell you that after experiencing her mentoring call and listening to all of her guess, I was overjoyed and full of excitement just to know that it was okay to LOVE MYSELF. Now, I was left with the memory of not knowing what was on the first night's call. I realized, that I still had some areas of closed mindedness. Isn't it just amazing that when we think that we have been transformed, God shows us that we can get a little closer to being what he has called us to be; loving our neighbor as we love ourselves? And this means we must first learn how to love ourselves- "love me some me."

Excuse me, I want to talk to a young woman and a young man right now. I want to speak into the lives of a teen boy or a teen girl right now. I do not know you, but I do KNOW that you are way more valuable and loved more than you could ever imagine. We must begin to love ourselves properly to the point that we perceive ourselves differently. We must began to feel that we are worth a million. We must think, believe and know that "I am made in the image and likeness of God."

Women, you must place Godlike worth over your mind, your emotions, your body and your soul. We as women, can no longer allow men to abuse us and think that it is acceptable. It is not acceptable, anytime or anywhere. Your worth is far above rubies. Teens, you can no longer allow anyone to bully you, call you names or look down on you. Ignore them! You must ignore those whose minds and mouth are untruthful. You must not define yourself by the opinions of others. Walk away from those who would abuse you. Set your boundaries in place. Began to love yourself. Start your healing journey towards wholeness. You are worthy to be loved. You are so valuable Go ahead and start the process of learning to love yourself.

I remember that day so well while Pastor Paula White was speaking and at the end of that demonstration, she said that we get so afraid to put on a $700 suit or a $1,000 dress because we do not feel that we deserve it. She said, "Some of you even feel funny just trying on a $1,000 dress." She said, "There is no crime in trying on an expensive outfit on."

YOU ARE VALUABLE

There is an army of ladies "rising up" who have concluded that they ARE worthy to put on such a garment and that THEY are valued for

WHO they are. You are a human being that has been created in the image and in the likeness of your God. Pastor Paula White declared that very day that no dress is worth more than her body. She said, "I make the dress look good." She said on that particular day that "the cloth that the dress is made from is not even worthy of my body." She "pressed in on the issue" that YOU ARE VALUABLE and a priceless jewel in the eyes of God.

If we are made in the image of God, then that is as high as it gets!

I am smiling right Now because I know that I am somebody. I know that I am loved; I know that I am blessed, and "I love me some me."

See, it has taken me way too long to come to this conclusion. Sometimes we get deceived in this world and we think that just because someone has mistreated us that we are worthless and not worth loving, but I am here to tell you that this is a lie. Just because that other person did not know your VALUE, or your WORTH did not mean that you were NOT who God has called you when you were born. God calls you SON, God calls you DAUGHTER.

Another author whom I read who helped me when I was going through trying to figure out the "Love issue" is the famous Iyanla Vanzant. She is an amazing woman, survivor of much emotional pain. She thrives in her new life. She knows what it means to lose love, feel hurt, ashamed and confused. Yet she GOT UP AGAIN AND HEALED HER HEART. She learned to forgive and to think properly. She learned to talk with power and authority. She learned to walk by faith. And she also learned how to love again. She unknowingly did my five steps. LOL!

In her book "In the Meantime-Finding yourself and the love you want"

On page 91 she talks about healing yourself emotionally and she states to stop picking on yourself. She states, "The healing process that leads you to the ultimate experience of self-love and unconditional love works whether or not you are involved in an intimate relationship. You can always stop what you are doing and check in on yourself. This would help you determine if you are moving through an experience toward healing or responding to the motivational influence of a toxic emotion. You need to know why you are doing what you are doing so that you can begin to clean house. This personal, internal, emotional housecleaning involves the removal of some junk, clutter, and trash in your mental and emotional closets."

I really appreciate her honesty and she states that this is a HEALING PROCESS. Here goes that word Process again. Going through the process does mean it will take a little time. It takes time to heal. It takes days, weeks, months, even years to heal some wounds. Healing comes with a price. The price is: you must want to be healed and start the process by working on yourself.

You may want to know how long it will take to work these FIVE steps.

I cannot tell you how long because everyone is different. If you do all of the five Steps you will begin to notice major changes in 90 days. Here is a short list to get you going NOW, TODAY: forgive myself and people, change my thinking to a positive vibration and start to talk with intention to create the outcomes I desire. How long will it take when I add using the step of Faith-step four and the step of Love-step five? Again you will see progress within 90 days. Some people will need to get into a support group so that they can finally practice all of the steps with encouragement. You can ask to be added to the private Facebook group called "Get up Again" for ongoing support.

Saturate yourself with love and learn how to love others properly, Agape love that is. I will tell you that there is no certain time frame, but just start your new journey as a new lifestyle and you will see gradual change. Adopt these "five steps" and make a commitment to stay the course and you will get the results you want. If you stick to it, you will become a transformed person and as life coach Lisa Nichols says, "Barely recognizable".

IT IS TIME FOR SOME EMOTIONAL HOUSE CLEANING

Believe me, the healing will come. I am a witness to the "Get Up-Heal your Heart process." My life is a continuation of learning and getting better. Let me invite you to meditate and enter into a place of rest. Allow the healing to come by getting the junk out of your mind. I like to say get the trash out of the kitchen or it will stink! Nobody really enjoys taking out the trash and especially cleaning out the trash can! But "Do It Anyway" as my business life coach, Zenovia Andrews would say!

Do your emotional house cleaning! Forgive the past and release old grudges and fears. Think on good and positive things. Speak empowering words over your life! Begin to walk the life of Faith! Then be willing to love yourself and Love others again!

I am changing my LIFE DAILY with this FIVE step process and I know it will change your life too!

You CAN get up again and have the life you deserve. Thank you for spending time reading my story and for listening to this wonderful process. You can start the five step program today. Let me help you get connected and get started in one of my programs.

Remember to get added to my private **Facebook page called WOMAN TO WOMAN-GET UP or Give Birth to Your Dreams group.**

If you need assistance, please contact me for private coaching or speaking engagements. I am also available for consults or group classes.

Feel free to inbox me or send me a message through face book on messenger.

I am here for you! Happy healing!

PAMELA HART

Bibliography

1. No Matter What!-9 Steps To Living the Life You Love-by Lisa Nichols

2. Boundaries-When to say Yes and when to Say No-by Dr. Henry Cloud and Dr. John Townsend

3. The Law of Confession-by Dr. Bill Winston

4. My Thoughts on Victorious Confessions-by Bridget E. Hilliard

5. Take Times for your Life-by Cheryl Richardson

6. Transform Your Thinking, Transform your Life-by Bill Winston

7. Maximize The Moment-God's Action Plan for your Life-by T.D. Jakes

8. Imagine Big-Unlock the Secret to living out your dreams-by Terri Savelle Foy

9. The Freedom Formula- How to put Soul in your Business and Money in your Bank-by Christine Kloser

10. The Business of Living by Dr. Jack H. Grossman

11. Self-Love-by Robert H. Schuller

12. 30 days to Taming your Tongue-by Deborah Smith Pergues

13. In the Meantime-Finding yourself and the love you want-by Iyanla Vanzant

14. May I have my order Please- by Pastor Rickie G. Rush

15. Daily Power of Prayer-by Dr. Myles Munroe

16. The Holy Bible-KJV and Message versions

www.ingramcontent.com/pod-product-compliance
Lightning Source LLC
Chambersburg PA
CBHW071143090426
42736CB00012B/2203